MW00614004

Endorsements

"The principles contained in this book are powerful and life-changing. When I first heard Pastor Ish teach them, my eyes were opened to the connection between physical disease and spiritual "dis-ease." I pray that reading and applying the truths of this book will bring you and those you love the relief it has brought to many in our church."

Miriam Callahan
Community Pastor
Bandera Road Community Church
San Antonio, Texas

Ish Payne has a true shepherd's heart. His teaching "living in the Red Zone" is helping multitudes in the body of Christ not only receive their inheritance of healing spiritually, emotionally, and physically, but it is also a practical guide in learning "how" to hold on to peace and maintain healing once the Lord's provision has been received. This book and understanding the "Red Zone" will help the reader connect the dots between the lack of peace one feels emotionally, and "dis-ease." This book is a must read for every Christian in order to overcome the challenges that are faced everyday, so the abundant life of health and peace can be enjoyed!

Rev. Deanne Day
Founder of Mending Hearts Ministries
Restoring Hearts International Team Member

"Life in the Red Zone" serves at least two major functions for the Body of Christ. The first is like a diagnostic center that helps clearly identify the source of a host of common "maladies" (areas of affliction in the soul and body) that too many people have learned to cope with, rather than deal with. The second is like a prescription for how to deal with the affliction...in other words, what to do about it! This material isn't "arm chair" theology. This is stuff that works, and actually helps in destroying the work of the devil in the lives of hurting people. I have known Ish and Tonda for many years. Ish is a servant to the Body of Christ, and has learned through serving how to bring the kind of knowledge to those in need that has the potential to renew the mind and bring transformation. His insight and ministry has helped transform people in my church, and with my prodding and encouragement, he has put in written form the pertinent lessons that he has learned. I strongly endorse this work, and look forward to hearing the powerful testimonies that will follow.

Steve Doerter
Senior Pastor
Grace Community Church
Cashiers, NC

Ish Payne is a man after the Father's heart. The "RED ZONE" reflects his passion for God's people. Ish has coined a timely and a relevant message that will empower believers to live above the anxiety and stress that traps so many people. I believe Ish and Tonda Payne are valuable assets to the Body of Christ because of their sensitivity to the anointing of the Spirit to set captives free. This book is the fruit of their life-long labors to bring healing and restoration to those who are broken-hearted and over-whelmed with the cares of this world.

Phillip Fields
Executive Director
Get Real Ministries
Point, TX
www.grministries.org

I thank God that He has given Ish a doctor's degree in the "school of hard knocks." It has been a real pleasure to share Ish's journey with him and absorb some of the lessons he has learned. All of us have something to overcome in life. Ish's book makes bible basics come alive so we can apply them more successfully. Thank you Lord for this man, his family, his ministry, his Kingdom work, and this book "Life in the Red Zone"!

Reid M. Henson
Vice Chairman (Retired)
Coca Cola Bottling Co. Consolidated

In reading over this book, "Life in the Red Zone", Pastor Ish Payne has given us through his training, life experiences, and what the Holy Spirit has revealed to him, the seriousness of "unrepented sin." "Sin" we don't realize, because satan has deceived us into believing that it is "Not Sin", such as, unforgiveness, bitterness, anger against someone who has hurt us, or self-bitterness, self-hatred, performance, perfectionism, envy, jealousy, comparison, worry, and the list goes on. When counseling with clients who have hurts from the past, we see that those sins have caused them pain, suffering and even disease. With the knowledge that Pastor Ish has given in his book, to avoid the "Red Zone", we as Christians, need to "repent" of those sins and let the Lord heal our hearts. God has shown Pastor Ish practical ways that we can maintain our lives and have "homeostasis" (peace) by repentance and forgiveness.

Rev. Donald W. McDonald, Ph.D
Patricia McDonald, Ph.D
Licensed Clinical Pastoral Counselors
Life Counseling Ministries
Atlanta, Georgia
www.lifecounselingministries.com

During my 10+ year journey out of the world of mainstream medicine, which focuses primarily on pharmaceutical drugs for treating symptoms of chronic degenerative diseases, I have continued to refine my wholistic and basic approach to achieving optimal health and "Temple maintenance." My more recent path has led me to discover the amazing and unsurpassed power of identifying and releasing toxic negative emotions through forgiveness and repentance. In fact, it now is the number one tenet which I teach for optimal health and wellness! Pastor Ish has, I believe, captured and related these amazing healing truths in his new book, Life in the Red Zone, in a very readable and understandable way. I urge anyone and everyone desiring optimal health and a vibrant victorious life to read and avail themselves of the healing power described so clearly and with such a sound biblical basis in these pages.

Franklin H. Ross Jr., M.D.
Integrated Health Care
Ashland, OR
www.drross4health.com

"Life in the Red Zone" by Ish Payne is an incredible teaching for the Body of Christ. It is a blend of facts from medical science balanced off with the promises of the Word of God. I believe "Life in the Red Zone" will bring the reader to freedom and to the pathway of wholeness from their past and even their present. Ish blends the Promises of God and teaches how to apply the Word to the very root of your need. I believe as you begin to study this book, you will begin to feel a release from your hurt and pain, and the past traumas and abuses that have happened to you in life. I believe this book is a tool to restore the peace of God, and bring healing and wholeness to your heart. May you experience the Father's love, divine health and truly understand that whom the Son sets free is free indeed

Pastor Wayne L. Shirk
New Hope Assembly
Saugus, Massachusetts

"I highly recommend "Life in the Red Zone"! Ish's military experience and his Marine training as a warrior has given him insight and understanding how to handle and teach the spiritual weapons that we must use to overcome the entanglements of this life (the Red Zone) in order to please Him who has enlisted us to be a soldier! (II Tim 2:2-5) I wish I had this teaching when I was younger!!" Every military man and woman will enjoy this book!

Major Franklin Therber (Ret)
Hendersonville, TN

LIFE IN THE
RED ZONE

Ish Payne

LIFE IN THE RED ZONE
© 2006 Ish Payne

ISBN: 0-9787246-0-7

Printed in the United States of America
1st Printing 2006

Cover Art and Design by Joseph Frye

"Scripture quotations marked "NAS" are taken from the New American Standard Bible®, Copyright © 1960, 1962, 1963, 1968, 1971, 1972, 1973, 1975, 1977, 1995 by The Lockman Foundation Used by permission." (www.Lockman.org)
Scripture quotations marked "AMP" are taken from the Amplified Bible, Copyright © 1954, 1958, 1962, 1964, 1965, 1987 by The Lockman Foundation. Used by permission.

Scripture quotations marked "NIV" are taken from the HOLY BIBLE, NEW INTERNATIONAL VERSION®. NIV®. Copyright© 1973, 1978, 1984 by International Bible Society. Used by permission of Zondervan. All rights reserved.

Scripture quotations marked "NKJV™" are taken from the New King James Version®. Copyright © 1982 by Thomas Nelson, Inc. Used by permission. All rights reserved.

ALL RIGHTS RESERVED
No part of this book may be reproduced in any form, stored in a retrieval system, or transmitted in any form by any means – electronic, mechanical, photocopy, recording, or otherwise – without prior written permission of the publisher.

Published by:
Restoring Hearts Ministries
PO Box 100
Indian Trail, NC 28079

Acknowledgements

Thank you Dr. Ben Haden of "Changed Lives Ministry" for showing me the difference between just going to the altar and true repentance! Years ago your example of love imparted to me a desire to serve our God and changed the course of my life!

To Pastors Michael & Melanie Hulsey, thank you for your apostolic hearts that desire to see other's dreams fulfilled. This project and book would never have happened without your vision and love!

To Pastors Steve & Joyce Doerter your encouragement to never give up or to look back has kept me going forward! Thank you for standing with us and believing in us!

To George Thrash, a true friend who has walked with me closer than a brother through the "good and the bad and the ugly" for many years. Thanks George!

To those special brothers who I consider my accountability partners – McLean Faw, Michael Hulsey, John Shergur, Steve Doerter, Peter DePaoli, David Savoie and Phillip Fields. In so many different ways you guys have kept me on track! Thank You!

To Reid Henson who is just a special friend! Thanks brother!

To Pastor Bonnie Chavda, a true mother in Israel and spiritual warrior, who is "Watching" over the flock. Tonda and I cannot thank you enough for your love and the time spent sharing His life!

To Tonda, my dear sweet wife, thank you for forgiving me for all the times I put you in the Red Zone! What we now know as the "Red Zone" is because of your spiritual insight and artistic ability to put in it a simple form that could be taught. I love you and praise God for you!

To my children, Joseph, Jason, Kelley, Taylor and Lexie you are the joy of my life and I thank you for loving on your dad! You have each made me so proud! May God bless your every thought and step!

To the Father, the Son and the Holy Spirit.....Your love has been poured out to me in ways that could not be contained in 1,000 volumes! My heart rejoices at the grace and love shown to me! I believe that this book is from your throne and I give unto you all the glory, all the honor and all the praise! Even as I type this tears of joy overflow at Your goodness to your creation! We bless Your name.

Contents

Foreword

Is living in 'the RED ZONE' killing you? Ish Payne's The Red Zone is a believer's handbook on personal well-being, the *homeostasis* the bible calls "peace." Ish has thoughtfully laid out the fundamentals of how you can live in God's complete peace. Mental, physical and spiritual *shalom* comes to us or evades us in direct correlation to what we think, what we eat and drink, and how we relate to others, beginning with God.

The Red Zone is a condensed and easy to use handbook that every home should have. From testimony (and humble openness) in his own life and heart, to the corroboration of science with scripture, Ish's joyful and straightforward presentation of the nefarious "red zone" (including his own encounters with loaded guns and rattlesnakes) is everyman's emergency prevention kit for the number one ailment of postmodern society: STRESS.

Learn how you can stay out of the 'red zone' of the effects of resistance from the enemy. Is it possible that you may be living under a 'self imposed curse'? The enemy will turn a foothold into a stronghold in an effort to kill, steal and destroy you and your loved ones.

Find out the power of your own free will combined with the promise of scripture will set you free to live in peace.

Ish and Tonda Payne practice what they preach. Ish says: "This is the hour of restoring hearts, not condemning them." This well researched book is great for pulpit presentation or home and personal bible study. Having walked in a healing ministry ourselves for over three decades and witnessing many miracles, we have also seen the great need for believer's to know how to walk in health as well as get healed! Based on the principles and power of the word of God, The Red Zone is an 'owner's manual' to living in health and peace.

Dr. Bonnie Chavda
Co-founder and Senior Pastor of All Nations Church and Executive Director of Mahesh Chavda Ministries

Introduction

Andrea was delighted!

Sitting on the porch having coffee with her mom, she was telling her that this was going to be the perfect day! She had just recently graduated from college and had gotten a job that she had wanted. Her hard work had paid off, and now she was going to be able to reap some of the rewards. She had enjoyed school, but it had not been easy carrying a full school schedule, while working at least thirty hours per week to support herself.

Today Andrea was going on a long hike with some of her friends, and tonight she was cooking a special meal for her family. She loved to cook and this was the first chance to cook for her family in almost a year.

Late that afternoon she went shopping at the big new super center. It was so crowded that she had to park quite a distance away, but hey, she was in shape and sure did not mind walking.

She did her shopping, returned to her car and put all the groceries in the trunk. She got in and headed down the freeway toward her home. It was at that moment that her day was shattered.

She looked into her rear view mirror to change lanes and saw a man rise up from the floor of the back seat holding a knife. She tried to scream, but it got stuck in her throat as the terror consumed her. She told me later that her first thought was that she was going to die, not from the knife, but from a heart attack! Her second thought was about her parents and how they were going to be able to deal with her death! Her third thought was that this was not happening, but was a dream or hallucination. But that thought was shattered when he grabbed her by the hair and held the knife to her throat! She was having trouble driving and she thought later that it would have been better to have wrecked. She knew a teenage girl had been abducted in this area, raped, and left for dead after her throat was cut! Was this the same man? Was this some kind of sick joke? She tried to remember if he had been caught.

She was shaking so badly that she could hardly keep her hands on the steering wheel or her foot on the gas. She had never known such fear! He then spoke for the first time and she saw that his teeth were rotten and his breath smelled of alcohol. He directed her to a secluded area and drug her out of the car by the hair and into the woods where he raped her.

She wanted to struggle and resist, but she was shaking so badly she had no strength. Afterwards he made her take him back to the same super center parking lot where he got out and ran around the side of the building.

As the police chaplain, I was on duty when the call came in that a 427 (sex crime) had been committed. The duty sergeant and I arrived at the same time to find this young gal really traumatized. An ambulance arrived shortly after and I rode with her to the hospital, because I knew that her ordeal was not over! I was so thankful for the staff at Erlanger Hospital; for I knew that they were very caring and sensitive with rape victims.

In the ambulance on the way to the hospital Andrea was starting to get mad and starting to blame herself for what had happened. She was also mad that after saving herself for her husband to be, that this smelly rotten toothed man had stolen something from her that could never be returned!

Shame from the degrading and humiliating experience was starting to settle in and she was having trouble looking anyone in the eye. Satan had gotten some strong "Footholds" through the door of this girl's life and he was trying to build stronger and stronger layers of destruction, which unless broken and dealt with would soon become "Strongholds"!

The experience was terrible, but the aftermath had all the potential to destroy the life of this sweet young gal. She had been the victim of someone else's gross sin, but her response to that sin would determine the outcome for her!

Would the fear, pain, anger, bitterness, distress, broken dreams, unfulfilled expectations, shame and guilt that start as "Footholds" become "Strongholds" that would rule and control her life?

Do fear, pain anger, distress, broken dreams, unfulfilled expectations, shame and guilt affect your life?

Would she be able to deal with these horrible "Footholds that can become Strongholds" that satan had put in her? Would she be able to pull down these "Footholds" that will define her life and even her identity?

Are you able to deal with these horrible "Footholds" that satan has placed in your life for the purpose of destroying you and stealing your joy?

Would you like to be able to destroy these "Footholds" before they become "Strongholds"?

Would you like to be free? I mean really, really free?

Free from those things that bind you!

Free from those things that keep you from proper relationships!

Free from shame and guilt over past experiences!

Free from anger and bitterness that has controlled your life and destroyed your health!

Free from the self pity that has isolated you!

I know you want to be free and that is why this book was written!

Freedom can be yours, and the Lord Jesus has shown us the way to get there! It was so simple that I missed it for years. Let me share it with you.

CHAPTER ONE

I'M CONCERNED! I AM REALLY CONCERNED!

Paul in writing to the Corinthian Church said: *"For though we walk in the flesh, we do not war after the flesh: For the weapons of our warfare are not carnal, but mighty through God to the pulling down of strongholds"* 2 Corinthians 10:3-4 KJV.

I'm concerned because we are engaged in a war, and very few people even know about it! Many people, including many Christians, are already captured and they don't even know it! When we don't know that there is a battle going and we are suppose to fight, then the enemy has already won!

There is an old adage that says "what we don't know can't hurt us". But that, of course, is a lie that the enemy has been telling us for 6,000 years! The scripture is very clear that *"My people are destroyed for lack of knowledge"* Hosea 4:6 KJV.

You could just as easily say my people have already lost and been taken prisoner, but use ignorance as an excuse. Sort of like a "Trojan Horse" experience! The enemy comes in and captures us, and we don't even know that he is there. Once he has access to your life through various *"footholds"* then he can continue to work his evil on you and in you and build, not one, but perhaps many

1

"strongholds". These *"footholds"* and *"strongholds"* create a condition in your life that I have named the **"Red Zone"**, and it is in the red zone that our bodies start breaking down!

According to my friends Peter and Toni Depaoli, directors of Reclaiming Victory Ministries in Aloha, Oregon a "Stronghold" is when you "Believe" the lie, and this only follows a "Foothold" which is when you "Listen" to the lie, and this only follows "Deception" which is "Hearing" the lie! Do you see the ugly progression?

#1 - **Deception** which is **Hearing** the Lie

#2 - **Foothold** which is **Listening** to the Lie

#3 - **Stronghold** which is **Believing** the Lie

You have to only look at Adam and Eve to see the stark reality of this truth! (Genesis 2&3)

Work of the Enemy!

We know that this is the work of the enemy that Jesus called the thief, when he said: *"The thief comes only in order that he may steal and may kill and destroy"* John 10:10 AMP.

Who is the target that the enemy is trying to steal from, kill and destroy? The answer is YOU! You are the target! Make no mistake about it, you are the target!

You see there are only two kingdoms in this world. One is the kingdom of God and the other is the kingdom of satan. There is no third kingdom!

Paul in writing to the Corinthian church regarding forgiveness said: *"To keep satan from getting the advantage over us; for we are not ignorant of his wiles and intentions"* 2 Corinthians 2:11 AMP. This warning must have been very important in Paul's mind, and if it was so important then God must be willing to show us how not to be ignorant. Don't you agree? You see Paul knew by experience

2

that satan wanted to hinder him from work in God's kingdom, and at times had thwarted him! He states it clearly: *"For we wanted to come to you—I Paul, more than once—and yet satan thwarted us"* 1 Thessalonians 2:18 NAS.

You see, it is vital for us to not only know and understand how God thinks, but also to know how the enemy thinks. We will learn both of these truths from the same book containing His holy word. The bible clearly teaches everything that is necessary for life and godliness. *"Grace and peace be multiplied to you in the knowledge of God and of Jesus our Lord, as His divine power has given to us all things that pertain to life and godliness, through the knowledge of Him who called us by glory and virtue, by which have been given to us exceedingly great and precious promises, that through these you may be partakers of the divine nature, having escaped the corruption that is in the world through lust"* 2 Peter 1:2-4 NKJV.

Jeremiah 29:11 – How God thinks!

One truth that must be settled in our hearts once and for all is found in Jeremiah:

"For I know the thoughts and plans that I have for you, says the Lord, thoughts and plans for welfare and peace, and not for evil, to give you hope in your final outcome" Jeremiah 29:11 AMP.

Take this scripture and put it on your refrigerator, bathroom mirror, dashboard of your car and any other place that will remind you of God's heart for you! In ministry I am often surprised how many people don't really know that their Father God loves them dearly and only wants the very best for them!

John 10:10 – How the enemy thinks!

Now we can see from the gospel of John that the message of the enemy is clear. Jesus said: *"The thief only comes in order that he may steal and may kill and may destroy. I came that they may have and enjoy life, and have it in abundance – to the full, till it overflows"* John 10:10 AMP.

Are you a war casualty?

Did anyone ever tell you that the enemy fights by his own rules and is out to destroy you in any way that he can?

Do you feel that life has passed you by and that you were dealt a bad hand of cards?

Did anyone ever tell you to leave the church following your divorce?

Do you feel rejected by the church, your family and friends because of your past or current failures, so that now you have withdrawn from just about everybody?

Do worship and praise songs get stuck in your throat?

Does everyone around you seem to be happy while you feel miserable?

When that person that wounded you walks into the room do you feel your face flush?

Are you hanging on by a thread afraid that at any time you are going to just lose it?

Are thoughts of "ending it all" becoming more commonplace in your mind?

If this sort of stuff is going on with you then you are living in the "Red Zone." Unless you get out of the "Red Zone" your body and mind will suffer because we were designed by our God to live in peace with Him, our neighbor and ourselves!

Is the Red Zone killing you?

Ok, first let's define what I am calling the "Red Zone"

God in designing us intended for us to live in peace! Jesus said

4

"Peace I leave with you, My peace I give to you: not as the world gives do I give to you. Let not you heart be troubled, neither let it be afraid" John 14:27 NKJV. There are many other scriptures to show that He wants us to live in peace and that He has even provided peace for us, just as He provided for our salvation and healing.

Isaiah wrote of Jesus *"Surely He has borne our griefs (sickness) and carried our sorrows (pains); Yet we esteemed Him stricken, Smitten by God and afflicted. But He was wounded for our transgressions. He was bruised for our iniquities (tendency to sin); The chastisement for our PEACE was upon Him, And by His stripes we are healed. All we like sheep have gone astray; we have turned every one, to his own way; and the Lord has laid on Him the iniquity of us all"* Isaiah 53:4-6 NKJV.

Would we agree that **salvation** *"(bruised for our iniquities, wounded for our transgressions")* and **healing** *"borne our grief, carried our sorrows and by His stripes we are healed"* were accomplished on the cross as spoken of here by Isaiah? Then if salvation and healing were accomplished, then so was our **peace** bought by Jesus *(by: the chastisement for our peace that was upon Jesus)*

Again, let's look at these powerful and life changing words spoken by the Lord Jesus: *"Peace I leave with you; My (own) peace I now give and bequeath to you. Not as the world gives do I give unto you. Do not let your heart be troubled, neither let it be afraid – stop allowing yourself to be agitated and disturbed; and do not permit yourself to be fearful and intimidated and cowardly and unsettled"* John 14:27 AMP.

Beloved, His **peace** is yours! He already paid the price! It is part of your inheritance in Christ! It belongs to you...... Take it!

Medical term – "Homeostasis" = peace

The medical community has a term for peace and it is *homeostasis*. According to the *Tabor's Cyclopedic Medical Dictionary* the word means: "State of equilibrium of the internal environment of the body that is maintained by the dynamic process of feedback and regulation." That is a nice medical term for what we simply know as **PEACE!**

The whole body was designed by God to function and live in **peace**, and when things go wrong, or we lose our **peace**, the body kicks in to bring us back to **peace**. How does the body kick in?

It kicks in through a process known as *Psychoneuroimmunology* (PNI)

Psychoneuroimmunology (PNI) is the fancy name that the medical community goes by as they are studying the mind/body connection. It is simply the interaction between the mind and the brain and the resulting changes in the hormonal or endocrine system which in turn has a dramatic effect on the body's immune system. Lets look a little closer at the way this works in our body.

The simplest and most concise definition that I have ever found was in a "Ladies Home Journal" article in November 2001 called "Mapping your stress points" written by Robin Uris. The writer, in describing how stress affects the body, states "It only takes a fraction of a second, whether it's thinking about work or a loud noise, to set off a chain reaction that affects everything from our eyesight to the muscles in our legs. The response begins in the brain, where the hypothalamus releases a fight-or-flight chemical called Corticotrophin Releasing Hormone (CRH). CRH travels to our pituitary gland, which secretes Adrenocorticotropin Hormone (ACTH), which travels to the adrenal gland on top of our kidneys. The result is adrenaline, a powerful stimulant. In an instant these changes occur...... vision sharpens, hearing improves, the thyroid speeds up, breathing becomes rapid and shallow, blood pressure rises, digestion slows, muscles tense and blood sugar rises"!

What she just described is the "Red Zone"! And it is the Red Zone that is making us sick and even killing us prematurely!

I had a doctor tell me recently "that 85 % of the people that came into his office with a problem were actually dealing with severe stress that manifested itself as a physical or emotional imbalance or disease".

Well, if stress is what puts us in the red zone then we need to define stress and the red zone.

Please take note of the red zone chart on the following page. This chart was developed by my wife Tonda and I in order to explain the medical and spiritual aspects of what is going on in our bodies. In teaching seminars I would try to explain it and use hand signals to illustrate it, but after a few times Tonda said "Ish no one knows what you are talking about" So she, being the artistic type, developed this red zone chart.

You see at the bottom of the chart an area that we show as peace or homeostasis. This, remember, is where God designed you to live, and when we start losing our peace, then, the stimulants start being released in order to try and bring the body back into home-ostasis. And as we saw from the definition, one of the main stimulants being released is adrenaline, and another one is cortisol.

Stress is really nothing more than tension! Random House Dictionary defines stress as physical, mental or emotional tension. I would also add to that definition that spiritual tension is also prominent!

Dr. London Smith, MD, writing in the early 1970's, said "that stress can be an exciting challenge to some and puts others to bed with a migraine, asthma or fever. Stress comes in many forms: emotional, allergic, surgical, physical, ecological. When a person perceives stress of any kind, the blood sugar falls, which signals the adrenals to secrete cortisol and adrenaline. Another factor that makes for adrenal gland exhaustion is the inefficient screening out of the victim's environment. He may *perceive stress* where the majority of his peers would feel comfortable. The world is too close and even threatening. The cortex of the brain reacts to overwhelm-

RED ZONE CHART

FIGHT
OR
FLIGHT

10	
9	

This is the dangerous stage.

Unforgiveness
Strife
Bitterness
Prolonged anxiety and stress
Unconfessed sin
Guilt
Shame

RESISTANCE

8	
7	
6	
5	
4	
3	

PEACE
"Homeostasis"

2	
1	

ing stimuli that other parts of the nervous system allowed to get through. The cortex assumes that attack is imminent and sends an SOS to the adrenals to pour out their hormones to prepare the body for fight or flight".

It is important to recognize that a perceived threat has just as much an effect on your system as a real threat. In fact, it is often the perceived threats that keep us tied up in knots. Such things as monthly bills, children's welfare, or even concerns about social security!

I have talked to a number of people who have worried themselves sick because they read that social security might not be here in 20 years! That is a perception at this time and is not a reality! That is why Jesus said: *"But seek first His kingdom and His righteousness; and all these things shall be added to you. Therefore do not be anxious for tomorrow; for tomorrow will care for itself. Each day has enough trouble of its own"* Matthew 6:33-34 NAS.

The Message translation says it like this: *"Give your entire attention to what God is doing right now, and don't get worked up about what may not happen tomorrow. God will help you deal with whatever hard things come up when the time comes"*.

Wow! That is powerful, and those are words from the Lord Jesus himself! Did He lie when He said those things? No! Jesus is clearly teaching us that our first priority is to *"seek first His kingdom"*. When we follow this admonition we will be at peace, for He promised to provide for all our needs and not to worry! For me this scripture promise means to let Him be the King. He is capable of taking care of all things and loves to do just that!

You see even a perceived threat or stressor will cause this reaction in your body. In a nutshell it really boils down to this cycle taking place in your body:

Emotions & behaviors > cause endocrine or hormonal changes > which affect the immune system. Some people have called this the mind/body connection, and the medical community certainly knows it is true! Praise God the church is beginning to understand this process and is taking their rightful place in ministering to the spirit, soul and body.

The evidence is non-debatable and undisputable that stress, or lack of peace, is making us sick and causing us to die prematurely. It has been confirmed by countless scientific and medical studies.

You see, the way we have designed the red zone chart is to show that there is a progression of issues that cause the numbers to rise. Actually, fight or flight would immediately start when stress begins, either real or perceived, but I have tried to illustrate the difference between low-level stress (if there is such a thing) and the stress of, say, running from a bear! You see, when we are running from a bear, or are in a dangerous situation, our bodies instantly prepare us for the emergency. That is why we have read those unbelievable stories of little grandmothers picking up cars off of their grandchildren. Now this only lasts for a few moments and the body will start returning to homeostasis.

A Cop Story

I had an experience when I was a policeman years ago that I like to relate to help illustrate what happens when fight or flight occurs.

I was on duty one night when a call came in that Officer Dick Roberts had stopped a drunk driver and needed back up. Dick and I had been friends in the Marine Corp and had served together in the Second Marine Division. I went to the scene and found Dick had stopped a man driving a large pick up truck for driving drunk. And this guy was really drunk and really big!

Dick and I knew that we had to get his keys out of the ignition and away from him as he was ready to drive off. He was so drunk

10

that he did not even recognize us as policeman, even though we had on uniforms and the cars blue lights were flashing. The guy was a mess, and dangerous not only to others, but to himself and us as well!

Ok, so Dick went around to the driver's door and was trying to get into the cab of the truck to get his keys out of the ignition as I was talking to him through the driver's door, which he had opened. Mostly I was just trying to avert his attention from Dick.

That's when it happened!

I was standing on the ground talking to this guy with the door open when I saw a flash of light and heard a loud muffler coming from the right or rear of the truck. I looked and saw that a vehicle was bearing down on us at a high rate of speed and I had no where to go! I jumped up onto the running board of the truck, and just as I did, this car, going probably 70 to 80 miles per hour, hit the left rear panel of the truck and came down the side of the truck taking the door off and throwing it far down the road. The car was literally only inches or less from my body, but totally missed me! The car was so close that I could feel the heat and fierce wind as it flew behind me! Not only that, but if the car had plowed into the truck no one would be around telling this story. It literally happened so fast that the only reaction I had was to jump up on the running board and get as close to the truck as I could.

At the time I did not sense any fear, but when I started getting into my police car later I found that I was shaking so badly that I had trouble getting my foot on the accelerator and my hands to work the ignition. Within a few minutes the shaking stopped, but I could tell that my blood pressure was out of sight for quite some time. That is what happens in the fight or flight syndrome!

Medically speaking the following things take place in what is called the *"Flight-or-Flight or alarm"* reaction. There is a stimulation of the sympathetic nervous system and the adrenal medulla which activates the following:

1-tremendous amounts of oxygen & glucose released to the brain, skeletal muscles and heart

2-increased heart rate

3-constriction of blood vessels in viscera and skin

4-dilation of blood vessels in brain & skeletal muscles

5-contraction of spleen

6-conversion of glycogen into glucose in the liver

7-sweat production increases

8-rate of breathing increases

9-digestion slows down

10-increased secretion of epinephrine & norepinephrine

No Control

Did I have to tell my body to do all of these things to prepare for this unexpected emergency? Did I have to go to school to learn how to make my body react to the danger? No! It did all on its own, because that is the way God created me! It is very important to understand that we have no control over these things taking place in our body. When the stressor appears (in this case the speeding car) it stimulates the hypothalamus in the brain to initiate the fight or flight syndrome.

Of course another stressor would be the fact that as a policeman you have to deal with a totally irrational drunk who is very dangerous, so my body was already in a minor state of fight or flight.

Now, I don't know an exact time frame, but if you stayed in this high alert for very long (8-10 on the chart) you would go into shock and die. Your body was designed this way only for emergencies, which are not supposed to happen every day.

Ok, if you are with me so far, let's look at the other part of this syndrome which is called the *"Resistance reaction"*. This is not an emergency so to speak, but possibly just everyday life. Again, the medical definition would be "unresolved stress, anxiety and fear. This causes the stimulation of the anterior pituitary gland and adrenal cortex which activates the following:

A hormone called ACTHRF is released which causes:
1-decreased connective tissue repair
2-loss of protein from cells
3-retention of sodium
4-elimination of H+ ions
5-water retention
6-acidic blood
7-lowered ph value
8-calcium is drawn from the bones
9-blood insulin levels increase

A stress hormone HGHRF is released which causes:
1-The liver to be affected

A stress hormone TRF is released which causes:
1-The thyroid to be affected

You know, when I see statements about damage to the connective tissue, I think about diseases such as the many types of *arthritis*.

And when I think about water and sodium retention, I think about *blood pressure problems and heart and kidney problems*.

It is common knowledge that the dreaded and common disease *osteoporosis* is caused by low levels of calcium in the bones!

And when I see that blood insulin increases I must consider *diabetes*.

13

Now, according to medical facts, all of these issues and many, many more are caused by living in the **resistance reaction**, which I am calling the **"Red Zone"**

Again let's refer to the article in the November 2001 edition of "Ladies Home Journal" written by Robin Uris. I just love this article, as it sums up much of the medical data in a format that I can understand and relate to, and I am sure that you can as well!

She has taken mountains of data and research and put it into a very simple form! We don't need to have a medical degree or spend days and hours poring over medical and scientific knowledge to understand and apply these truths.

She says "We all have stress. Traffic. Taxes. A husband who can't find the dishwasher. Crying babies. Failed relationships. A looming deadline at work. But when stress snowballs it can take a serious toll our bodies.

Stress can cause our hair to fall out, our bodies to stop menstruating, and our joints to ache. It can lower the effectiveness of vaccines. A recent study by the Harvard University School of Public Health, in Boston, found that a stressful job can be as harmful to a woman's heart as smoking. Another, by Swedish researchers, concluded that women with marital stress are significantly more likely to suffer heart disease

"The trouble starts when the body is subjected to constant stress", says Richard Shelton, MD a professor at Vanderbilt University Medical Center, in Nashville, Tennessee. "The fight-or-flight response is supposed to be brief. But that's often not the case anymore. Acute stress has given way to chronic stress which can be harmful.

"This kind of constant stress can cause permanent damage by attacking each of us at our particular weak points. It can make us more susceptible to bothersome illnesses, like the common cold, and potentially fatal ones, like cancer. Researchers believe 80 percent of all diseases are linked to or aggravated by chronic stress", says Georgia Witkin, author of *The Female Stress Syndrome*.

Ok, now let's look at a condensed list of diseases that can be caused by living in the Red Zone. Again I want to give Robin Uris and Georgia Witkin credit for their fine work in compiling this list!

BRAIN: Stress begins in the brain, with a surge of hormones causing intense alertness. In this hyped state, we can't relax or sleep. But our minds can't function at this extreme level for prolonged periods. Eventually the hormone surges, and exhaustion cause tension headaches, irritability, aggression, inability to concentrate and memory loss.

"Unchecked stress can also trigger depression, which strikes twice as many women as men. Stress suppresses the hypothalamus, the emotion control center in our brains, curbing the production of the hormones that energize us and make us feel joyful." Says Witkin.

EARS: The surging hormones induced by stress improve our hearing to help us react to danger. But better hearing can actually be bad for the body. A recent Cornell University study concluded that even moderate noise elevates heart-damaging stress hormones. Studies have also shown that a lot of small noisy stressors added together such as honking horns, ringing telephones, and loud co-workers, can be more dangerous to the body than one major stressful event.

LUNGS: One of the first things we do when we feel stressed is hyperventilate. It's part of the body's fight-flight-response - in case we are in danger and need the extra oxygen in our bloodstream to run for cover. Those quick breaths can cause dizziness and sharp pains in the diaphragm. Severe stress can aggravate asthma and other dangerous respiratory conditions.

EYES: The adrenaline rush from stress dilates the eyes, improving vision. But it also triggers eye ticks because eye muscles

15

become fatigued. Eyes bulge if stress over stimulates the thyroid gland.

MOUTH: Dry mouth, bad breath and difficulty swallowing occur when stress makes us take short, shallow breaths. Under constant stress, some people clench their jaws or grind their teeth.

HAIR: Considered a barometer of inner health, hair is often the first to suffer. A body under stress burns nutrients, like the vitamin selenium, and that leads to dull hair and premature graying. Chronic stress can trigger the autoimmune system to attack hair follicles, causing hair to fall out completely or in clumps.

HEART: A heart under stress pumps fast and hard. Blood pressure rises as the body produces the hormones epinephrine and cortisol. That can lead to heart palpitations and chest pains. In those with heart disease, stress can prevent blood from clotting properly and stimulate the formation of plaque, and plugs arteries. Researchers say that even thinking about something stressful raises blood pressure. And a Swedish study concluded that stressful romantic relationships were more damaging to a woman's heart than work related stress. Women in troubled marriages were three times more likely to be hospitalized with heart problems.

IMMUNE SYSTEM: Ever get sick after a stressful event? Extreme and constant stress lowers our white blood cell count, making us more susceptible to disease and hampering our body's ability to heal itself. One recent study showed that the pneumonia vaccine was less effective in people under constant stress. Meanwhile, researchers are studying the link between stress and autoimmune disorders like Graves' Disease, in which the antibodies attack the thyroid, eye muscles and skin.

JOINTS, MUSCLES AND BONES: At tense moments, our brain sends messages to the muscles, tightening them and preparing them for action. Chronic stress can aggravate rheumatoid arthritis, cause sore muscles, and make us prone to sprains. Women who suffered chronic stress had lower bone density, according to a 1996 study published in the *New England Journal of Medicine.*

REPRODUCTIVE SYSTEM: Stress can halt menstruation, inhibit ovulation and cause premature birth and loss of libido. Doctors speculate stress-related infertility is the body's way of keeping us from becoming pregnant and giving birth under dangerous conditions. A University of California study showed that the stress hormones released by a pregnant woman can make her baby more prone to stress and the accompanying risk of heart attack. Stress may also contribute to the inability to achieve orgasm and may cause painful sex and premenstrual syndrome

SKIN: Stress causes hormones to be released that make acne, rashes, and itchy patches worse. Some people blush, while others go pale when the small blood cells in the skin contract. Under extreme stress, people can become covered in hives. "Any skin problem will get worse when you are stressed" says Jim Baral, M.D., a dermatologist at Mt. Sinai Hospital in New York City.

DIGESTIVE SYSTEM: Under stress, the brain shifts blood flow away from the digestive tract, which slows digestion. The result: indigestion, diarrhea, constipation, incontinence and colon spasm. Stress increases acid production, aggravating ulcers. It is also linked to colitis and irritable bowel syndrome, painful and sometimes debilitating digestive disorders. "Stress can be linked to digestive problems, so we routinely question patients about their life when taking a history of their symptoms" says Tarun Mullick, M.D., a gastroenterologist at The Cleveland Clinic, in Ohio

This information has become so commonplace that hardly a week goes by that I don't find confirming articles in newspapers, magazines and the web. Again, the evidence that stress causes serious issues in our mind and body is undisputable and undeniable.

17

CHAPTER TWO

SPIRITUAL STRESS

Now we have seen the physical and mental aspects of stress, but we need to define it in more spiritual terms.

What is spiritual stress? Basically they are issues that are caused by broken relationships between God, ourselves and others! What do we mean by this?

Well, Jesus summed it up when a lawyer asked him the question *"Teacher, which is the great commandment in the law?" Jesus said to him, "You shall love the Lord your God with all your heart, with all your soul, and with all your mind. This is the first and great commandment. And the second is like it: You shall love your neighbor as yourself. On these two commandments hang all the Law and the Prophets"* Matthew 22:36-40 NKJV.

If Jesus stated that this was so important, then we had better pay attention! He is saying that all the law and prophets hang on this scripture because He knew that our peace, happiness and abiding joy was wrapped up in these relationships with God, self and others.

Relationship with God

First, God created us to have fellowship with Him. Anything that breaks or hinders our fellowship with Him is going to put us in conflict with God, and how can we have peace with God if we are in conflict with God. Well we can't, and therefore our fellowship is broken and we lose our peace.

Simultaneously as our peace is lost we move into the resistance stage of fight-or-flight and that is the red zone. This resistance stage now causes the hormones cortisol and adrenalin to be secreted in our bodies that, left unchecked, will start breaking down our immune system by killing B cells and T cells.

So what is the answer? Simple, get back in proper relationship with God!

Well, how do we do that? We ask Him to show us where we went astray and then we just move accordingly to His voice! Jesus said it clearly: *"My sheep hear my voice, and I know them, and they follow me"* John 10:27 KJV.

James made it very clear that He will hear us and answer us when he said: *"But if any of you lacks wisdom, let him ask of God, who gives to all men generously and without reproach, and it will be given to him"* James 1:5 NAS.

Our Father God loves to talk to us and have fellowship with us in the same way we are excited when our own children seek us out for fellowship or advice.

A few years ago while on a ministry trip to Alaska, I went on a morning walk in the dark and cold. I was praying as I was walking, and I asked the Lord this question. "Lord, what do you want from me, and what do you want me to do"? I was struggling with some serious life decisions and had been seeking my Father God for the answers. You know that type of question where you want God to tell you exactly what to do, how to do it, and when to do it. He rarely answers those questions the way we would like for Him to, and His answer that morning was no exception.

He answered my question with a question of His own. "Ish, what do you want from your two little girls"? At the time Taylor was 13 and Lexie was almost 10. I pondered the answer only a second and said "Lord, I don't care if they ever make straight A's or be the star of anything. I just want them to know that I love them, and want them to be comfortable coming and sitting on my lap and talking to me about the things of their heart. I want them to know that they are always safe with me, and that I am always here for them"

The Lord immediately spoke to me and said these precious words. **"Ish that is all I want from you. I just want for you to come and sit on my lap and share your heart, and for you to know that you are safe with Me"**

Beloved, fellowship with God is not complicated. It is just a matter of coming and sitting on His lap and sharing your heart with Him.

Remember the Lord said *"Delight in me and I will give you the desires of your heart"*, *"I desire to establish you with all my heart and soul"*, *I am the Father who comforts you in all your troubles"* and *"When you are brokenhearted I am close to you"* Psalm 37:4, Jeremiah 32:41, II Corinthians 1:3-4, Psalm 34:18.

Relationship with others

I remember a dear elderly lady and her husband called me one day to ask questions about her physical condition. She was struggling with a terminal illness, and one of her buddies had told her that bitterness coming out of a broken relationship could set her up for the disease.

The three of us talked for some time and I explained that often bitterness towards God, self or others would cause our adrenalin and cortisol to over-secrete, and that process destroyed B cells and

T cells, and those were important components of our immune system. I explained the red zone to her and told her that my ministry experience showed that when this bitterness was there that it could wreak havoc in our bodies.

She agreed with that, and said that although she had not seen some of her friends over the years, she was not bitter towards anyone. Wonderful was the relationships she shared with her pals. She allowed me to ask her some questions, so I asked her about her husband (who was on the conference call), and she replied that they had been married for a very long time and that she had no issues toward him. He was very supportive of her and always had been. She also was a church leader, so I asked about relationships there as well. She reported no problems. We then went through children and grandchildren, and there again all the relationships were sweet and intact.

I was not sure where to go at that point, and suddenly I realized we had not discussed any siblings. So I asked her about her siblings. Did you have any? "Yes.", she replied "I have two sisters, but I have not seen them for over twenty years". Immediately in my mind I assumed that these two sisters were probably in a foreign land serving as missionaries. Why else would this sweet Christian lady not have seen her two sisters for over twenty years? I almost passed over it, but then I asked the key question—why? She replied that the sisters lived only 40 miles away, but twenty years ago their mother had died and that they had gotten into a big argument over the mother's silver tea set and had not spoken since!

Yikes! Up jumped the rabbit!

She had been carrying bitterness and unforgiveness for over twenty years and did not even recognize it!

Beloved, this is what I am calling a spiritual issue, and it will put you in the "red zone"!

Why was it a spiritual issue? Because she was out of relationship with her sisters and that put her out of relationship with God

Why? Simple! Because God commanded us to forgive others as He has forgiven us.

The Lord's Prayer

In the Lord's Prayer Jesus taught his disciples about forgiveness saying: *"And forgive us our debts, as we also have forgiven (left, remitted and let go of the debts, and given up resentment against) our debtors. And lead (bring) us not into temptation, but deliver us from the evil one. For Yours is the kingdom and the power and the glory forever, Amen"* Matthew 6:12-13 AMP.

An often overlooked scripture follows the Lord's Prayer when our Lord Jesus said: *"For if you forgive people their trespasses (their reckless and willful sins, leaving them, letting them go and giving up resentment), your heavenly Father will also forgive you. But if you do not forgive others their trespasses (their reckless and willful sins, leaving them, letting them go and giving up resentment), neither will your Father forgive you your trespasses"* Matthew 6:14-15 AMP.

This is certainly a sobering scripture quoting the Lord Jesus!

Does it mean that you lose your salvation if you don't forgive? No, I don't think so, but it definitely opens you up to an attack by the enemy, and it is certainly a sobering statement that we cannot ignore! Paul made it clear that we can open ourselves up to the enemy's attack when he said: *"nor give place (an opportunity) to the devil"* Ephesians 4:27 NKJV. I see that these scriptures about not forgiving are relating to the torment that is described in Matthew 18. This is the story of the man who, after having been forgiven an enormous debt, refused to forgive a friend's small debt, and consequently he was turned over to the tormentors. Matthew 18:21-35

The red zone is torment!

Think about it. Have you ever known anyone who was holding bitterness, resentment, unforgiveness, anger and malice toward another person?

Were they happy people? People full of joy and loving life?

No! They were miserable because all they could think about was the downfall of the person they were angry with.

Their life was consumed with evil intent towards their offender!

Is that a fun way to live?

No! It truly is torment, not only for you, but for all the people around you!

The writer of Hebrews said it well: *"Pursue peace with all men, and holiness, without which no one will see the Lord: Looking diligently lest anyone fall short of the grace of God; lest **any root of bitterness** springing up cause trouble, and by this many become defiled"* Hebrews 12:14-15 NKJV.

Can it be any clearer? The writer is telling us that bitterness is a violation of God's nature and when we entertain it we are asking for trouble, not only for ourselves, but also for those around us. Who are those around us? The answer, of course, is our families, our friends, our fellow workers; those that we are in contact with often. Those that we care about the most are being defiled by our bitterness!

Remember, Jesus said to forgive others as we have been forgiven. Jesus was establishing an eternal principle in saying that "forgiveness" should be extended even to those who don't deserve it.

Is that easy? No!

But by His grace we can do it. Jesus himself is our example!

The apostle Paul also made it clear in writing to the Ephesians church when he said: *"And be kind to one another, tenderhearted, for-*

24

giving one another, just as God in Christ forgave you" Ephesians 4:32 NKJV. He confirmed this principle again when writing to the Colossians he said: *"Therefore, as the elect of God, holy and beloved, put on tender mercies, kindness, humility, meekness, longsuffering; bearing with one another, and forgiving one another, if anyone has a complaint against another; even as Christ forgave you, so you also must do"* Colossians 3:12-13 NKJV.

You see to make a choice contrary to the established principles and the established will of God would put us into an adversarial position with God and therefore our minds and bodies would go into the red zone. And it is in the red zone where we are susceptible to torment and disease!

A self imposed curse?

When we read Deuteronomy 28 we find vivid evidence that our obedience or disobedience can and will bring about consequences. Verses 1 through 14 declare what blessings are ours when we hear and obey. However verses 15 through 68 are also a clear declaration of the results of not listening and not obeying! I would encourage you to read this slowly and really meditate on what these scriptures are saying.

Some might say, "Well that is old testament"! No! That is why I am encouraging you to read and meditate. You will find that the New Testament is teaching the same thing. The difference is that under the new covenant we have the Holy Spirit living in us that will enable and empower us to walk as God desires. Beloved, that is the same Holy Spirit that raised our Lord Jesus from the dead! Yes! Hallelujah!

These are not statements to bring us into condemnation, but clear teachings to help us know the heart of the Father and His desire for us. Beloved, it is all about choices! Are we going to choose life and blessing, or are we going to choose disobedience and cursing? To abide in Him we must hear His voice and then be obedient. (John 14:21-24) Sounds really simple, doesn't it? **The problem is that it is very difficult to be pursuing the Lord's kingdom, when we are so absorbed in our own!** That is part of the carnal thinking we will address later.

Joy Dawson, in her book on hearing and obeying the voice of the Lord "Forever Ruined for the Ordinary," makes a classic statement when she says: "God keeps all of His promises! Disobeying Him is the same as telling Him to hold back all the blessings that come with obedience, and bring on all the punishments that come with disobedience! That is not only stupidity, that's insane. Because of who God is, it is not only the height of preposterous pride to disobey Him, it is totally illogical"

Joy Dawson, Forever Ruined for the Ordinary (Seattle, Washington; YWAM Publishing, 2001 page 135.) Used with permission.

Again from Deuteronomy the lord says: "I call Heaven and Earth to witness against you today: I place before you Death and Life, Blessing and Curse. Choose Life so that you and your children will live. And love the Lord your God, listening obediently to Him, firmly embracing Him. Oh yes, He is life itself, a long life settled on the soil that God, your God promised to give your ancestors, Abraham, Isaac, and Jacob" Deuteronomy 30:19-20 The Message.

Another true story is about a pastor from the mid-west who was asking me if bitterness could have anything to do with the debilitating illness that he suffered with. I shared that my experience in ministry and medical documentation would confirm that bitterness can definitely be a cause. But regardless if bitterness was the cause for the disease there was no doubt that entertaining bitterness in your life was to live in the red zone, and to live in the red zone would have negative effects on your immune system. I further explained that disease attacks a weakened immune system, so we want to deal with any red zone issues that are hindering our immune system, in order that our body can fight the way God designed it to.

This casual meeting over coffee quickly turned into a ministry session as he kept asking questions. He shared that he had no bitterness in his life. He had had some issues from wounding while serving in another church, but those were now settled through forgiveness. He was fine with all his family members including his wife and children.

Suddenly he said to me: "Would it make any difference if I hated one of my in-laws?

Wow, again up jumped the rabbit!

This hatred and bitterness was there and had been there for many years, yet he did not even see it as a problem! He had justified his feelings because of the multiple offenses that had been caused by this family member. He was calling his feelings nothing more than normal emotions, but he soon saw that they were actually a sin issue, as he was in disobedience to the command of his savior to forgive!

Well, now I knew that, regardless of the disease issue, he had a bitterness issue that was keeping him in the red zone and that it was constantly having a negative impact on his immune system.

Remember that our bodies react involuntarily to an alarm reaction (fight-or-flight). The reaction is as normal as breathing! We can't control it and we can't stop it until we deal with the issues that are causing the alarm reaction.

Other Alarm Reaction Issues

Some other issues that we see often causing an alarm reaction are **guilt, shame, fears, grief, sorrow, unfulfilled expectations, broken dreams, performance to please someone - usually a father or mother- rejection, jealousy, gossip, slander** and many others.

27

All of these issues put us in the red zone and cause our immune systems to be compromised.

That was the only conversation we had concerning the subject, but I found out later that he had been healed of the illness and gave credit for his healing to understanding the principles of forgiveness and repentance.

You see, the Lord Jesus puts high priority on his word! In fact, it says in the Psalms that *"For you have magnified your word above all your name"* Psalms 138:2B NKJV.

God is guarding His word not only to perform it, but to see if we will guard it as well!

This is not legalism! This is hearing His voice and doing it, clear and simple!

James said: *"But be doers of the word and not hearers only, deceiving yourselves. For if anyone is a hearer of the word and not a doer, he is like a man observing his natural face in a mirror: for he observes himself, and immediately forgets what kind of man he was. But he who looks into the perfect law of liberty and continues in it, and is not a forgetful hearer but a doer of the work, this one will be blessed in what he does"* James 1:22-25 NKJV.

Do you want to be blessed?

Well here is a key to blessing! *"Be ye doers of the word and not hearers only"* James 1:22 NKJV. What a precious promise!

Do you want to be the friend of Jesus?

Jesus told us how to be His friend through the apostle John when He said: *"You are my friends if you do whatever I command you"* John 15:14 NKJV.

Do you want to bear much fruit for the Lord?

He tells us how in John when He said: *"I am the vine and you are the branches. He who abides in Me, and I in him, bears much fruit: for without me you can do nothing"* John 15:4 NKJV.

Relationship with Yourself

A bad relationship with yourself, or not liking yourself, may well be the biggest issue of all. This seems to be particularly true with Christians! That does not seem possible, but I have seen it literally hundreds of times. In fact, I have seen it so much that I would have to say that *"self hatred"* or *"self bitterness"* is a Christian plague! Peter and Toni Depaoli directors of Reclaiming Victory Ministries; Aloha, Oregon call this a spirit of *"self opposition!"*

The reality is that when you are down on yourself, you are in the red zone and your immune system is being compromised. This is true primarily because when you are down on yourself you are usually dealing with shame and guilt! This not only affects the body, but the mind as well.

Little Susie

I never met Little Susie, but she called me one day to ask questions about a disease that she was suffering from. Now, Little Susie was in her early forties and was a born again, spirit filled Christian and a leader in her church. She was not a novice in the Lord and had a real heart for people and the Lord's kingdom.

She had heard that there was a possibility that bitterness could be the cause of the disease. Knowing that it is an indisputable fact that bitterness can cause illness, I began asking her questions about her relationships. I questioned her about her husband, her children, her parents, her in-laws, her pastor and her fellow workers. She assured me that her relationship with all these family members was fine. I believed her. Usually you find some relationships that are out of kilter, but in her situation nothing was uncovered.

Then I realized that she had not told me what disease she was suffering from. After asking her, she explained that she had an auto immune disease and that she was first diagnosed with it in her late thirties.

Well, now I knew to look for "self bitterness", as ministry experience said that when you do not like yourself (self hatred or self opposition) that your body will start attacking itself! Again, another round of questions, but those questions didn't reveal anything either. I was getting a little frustrated and we were about to hang up when the Lord prompted (word of knowledge) me to ask her this question.

Now readers, as I tell you the question that I asked her, ask yourself the same question, and be honest about the answer because it may reveal a lot.

Ok, here is the question!

I said "Susie, when you stand before the mirror in the morning and you see yourself, what do you think about yourself?"

Ok. Did you ask yourself that same question? "When you stand in front of the mirror what do you think about yourself?"

She said "Oh! Ish, that is easy. I always think the same thing. As I look at myself, I think I wish I were dead!" Yikes! Up jumped the rabbit again!

Now I know this gal well! Oh yes, I know her well! Why do I know her?

"For out of the abundance of the heart the mouth speaks" Matthew 12:34b NKJV.

"For as he thinks in his heart, so is he" Proverbs 23:7 AMP.

"For death and life are in the power of the tongue" Proverbs 18:21 KJV.

"You are snared by the words of your mouth" Proverbs 6:2 NKJV.

The scriptures are our teachers, and they have everything that we need for life and godliness and they have just revealed this dear sister's heart!

Spirit of Death!

I learned two very important things by her statement. First, I learned that she hates herself for some reason. Second, I learned that she has been entertaining a *spirit of death*! That spirit of death desired to kill her and was doing a good job of it.

Remember Jesus said that *"the thief (satan) does not come except to steal, and to kill, and to destroy"* John 10:10a NKJV. The thief's mission is to kill, make no mistake about that!

You see this dear Christian gal had been tricked by the deceiver and everyday she had been cursing herself with the words "I wish I were dead"! And the thief had taken her up on her wish! So now she had a spirit of death and infirmity and she was enforcing its position with her constant confession that she wanted to die.

Jesus healed and delivered a dear woman with a spirit of infirmity in the Luke account of the gospels. *"Now He was teaching in one of the synagogues on the Sabbath. And behold, there was a woman who had a spirit of infirmity eighteen years, and was bent over and could in no way could raise herself up. But when Jesus saw her, He called her to Him and said to her "Woman you are loosed from your infirmity". And He laid His hands on her, and immediately she was made straight and glorified God"* Luke 13:10-13 NKJV.

You see that spirit of death was a spirit of infirmity that was trying to **steal** from her, **kill** her and **destroy** her, but our Lord Jesus was there to heal and deliver!

Somehow this woman had been plagued with a spirit of infirmity and no amount of counseling was going to set her free. She needed a divine impartation from Jesus the Son of the living God and she got it!

31

Beloved, this is divine healing and deliverance. And Jesus has given unto us the believer the same power and authority to heal the sick and cast out demons. Yes, thank you Lord!

Little Johnny

Ok, so how did Susie get into this situation where she was daily cursing herself? Well, little Johnny was the one who broke her heart and it happened at the tender age of 12.

She shared that Johnny had invited her to the junior high prom which was her first real social event. Susie and her mother had made a beautiful dress and made all the special preparations for the big event.

The problem was that Johnny stood her up and took another young girl. Susie was just devastated! They lived in a small town that only had one junior high school and everybody knew what had happened. She was so broken up by the experience that she was unable to go to Sunday school and church the following morning, because of flu like symptoms. That is a demonstration of just how fast our immune system can crash after a traumatic event. It has happened to me, and probably has happened to you as well. Medically and scientifically it happens because the traumatic experience dramatically lowers our white blood cell count.

Susie said that following this rejection and humiliation was when she started looking at herself in the mirror and wishing she was dead. You see, the thief had convinced her that she was not pretty or special. In fact, that accusing spirit told her that even though she was a youth leader in her church and a leader in her school that she was not significant, because Johnny had taken another girl! She quickly developed a hatred for herself that was still a major part of her identity after all of those years.

You may think that Susie became a recluse and was never seen again. Quite the opposite, she was still a leader in the same church and now a community leader married to a fine man, and they had two wonderful children. From all appearances she was on top of the world and had everything together. Underneath the smile was a gal that was still trying to be special and unique, but had believed a lie from hell that she was neither!

We wear many masks

I know from telling this story in many seminars and conferences that many of us are just like Susie. The details may be different, but the outcome is still very similar.

We learn to put on the face that we think everyone wants to see, which is aptly called a "fabricated personality". Without the grace of God working in our lives we can go to our grave with a mask on, which is a fabricated personality. It is sometimes too painful to face the perception that we are not unique and special, and so we spend our whole lives pretending to be something else.

The enemy gets a "foothold" when we listen to a lie, and then he gets a "stronghold" when we believe the lie! That is exactly what happened to this young gal. Do you see the progression? First, the enemy gets us to listen to him instead of God, and when we choose to listen to the wrong voice it can quickly become a "stronghold".

Beloved, ask the Lord to expose the lie and get a hold of the truth that the Lord has made each of us and we are all unique and special and greatly loved!

Let's just look at few scriptures that define God's great love for us.

"Before I formed you in the womb, I knew you" Jeremiah 1:4 NAS.

"In Him we also were made and we obtained an inheritance; for we had been foreordained (chosen and appointed beforehand) in accordance

with His purpose, Who works out everything in agreement with the coun-sel and design of His (own) will" Ephesians 1:11 AMP.

"For you did form my inward parts, You did knit me together in my mothers womb" Psalm 139:13 AMP.

"For I am fearfully and wonderfully made" Psalms 139:14 NAS.

"How great is the love the Father has lavished on us, that we should be called the children of God" I John 3:1 NIV.

"For I know the plans I have for you", declares the Lord, *"plans to prosper you and not harm, plans to give you hope and a future"* Jeremiah 29:11 NIV.

"The Lord is near to the brokenhearted, and saves those who are crushed in spirit" Psalm 34:18 NAS.

"This is love: not that we loved God, but that he loved us and sent His son an atoning sacrifice for our sins" I John 4:10 NIV.

"For I am convinced that neither death, nor life, nor angels, nor prin-cipalities, nor things present, nor things to come, nor powers, nor height, nor depth, nor any other created thing, shall be able to separate us from the love of God, which is in Christ Jesus our Lord" Romans 8:38-39 NAS.

"For God so loved the world that He gave His only begotten Son, that whoever believeth in Him should not perish, but have everlasting life" John 3:16 KJV.

If God loves you who else matters?

Some of you are saying, "Yeah right! You try living your life with no one loving you, or thinking no one loves you and see how it feels." Well, I did that very thing for the first 40 years of my life and it was miserable, and it kept me in the "red zone", and brought me untold anguish in body and mind. The worst part was that I didn't even know it. Many people cared and loved me deeply, but my perception was that they didn't. That is called deception!

Truly, often we are perishing for lack of knowledge! The prophet Hosea said *"My people are destroyed for lack of knowledge. Because you have rejected knowledge, I will also reject you from being priest for me; because you have forgotten the law of your God, I will also forget your children"* Hosea 4:6 NKJV. Isaiah confirmed this when he wrote *"Therefore my people have gone into captivity, because they have no knowledge; their honorable men are famished, and their multitude dried up with thirst"* Isaiah 5:13 NKJV.

All of the well known psychologists agree that every human has at least 3 basic needs. Those three needs are:

need to be loved
need to be safe and secure
need to be significant

A recent headline in the Charlotte Observer says *"Broken Hearts Equal Sick Bodies and Minds"*. The article was stating that psychologists and psychiatrists are seeing more and more the connection with "broken hearts" and diseases of the body and mind.

Well, the Bible has been teaching it for a long time. A broken heart comes out of a broken relationship, emotional wounding, and betrayal. Effective ministry will help you identify those broken relationships in order that you can experience healing!

But any therapy or counseling that does not bring you to Jesus is superficial at best. There are many fine people trying to help others, but the only real help is helping you find yourself in the arms of Father God. That relationship with "Abba" supersedes all others.

I certainly agree with these psychologists, but I would disagree about how to achieve it. You see, the psychologists have you running around all the bases, but you never get home! Why? Because many of them don't know where home is!

Home Plate

Home is in the Father, Son and the Holy Spirit! Well documented are the countless people who have chased the bases only to find that they were going in circles!

Beloved, chasing bases puts you in the "red zone" and is an open door to all kinds of maladies!

You see, Susie falsely believed that Johnny and others were her happiness and contentment. But that was a lie! Even though she partially recovered and went on with her life she was still trapped by the trauma of that humiliation experience! You see, no man or woman, job, car, house, church, position, or money will ever fill the need that was designed by God to fill. Only the God who created you to have fellowship with Him can fill the void that you were born with. This is why God made it clear that *"You shall have no other gods before me"* Exodus 20:3 NKJV. The correlation in the New Testament would be the words of Jesus *"Seek first the kingdom of god and His righteousness, and all these things shall be added to you"* Matthew 6:33 NKJV.

An age old problem is that people look to and believe that another person can fill those great needs that only the Lord can fill. Jimmy Evans said it like this, while teaching on the principle of transference: "Whenever we don't trust Jesus to meet our deepest needs we transfer expectations to others, and usually that is our spouse or the ones closest to us".

When we are depending on others to meet our needs we will be in a state of constant frustration, because our inner security depends on someone we can't predict or control! The only one predictable is the Lord who promised not to change and to love us unconditionally.

We become easily offended and bitter because no one can meet

36

these needs, and we are constantly blaming them for their short-comings, when the reality is that only the Lord can meet our needs.

It is no wonder that so many marriages fail! We are looking in the wrong places (people, places and things) for our happiness and joy, and only finding frustration, bitterness, discouragement and cynicism.

Our God is a jealous God and He is not pleased when we give His glory to another. *"I am the Lord, that is my name; And My glory I will not give to another"* Isaiah 42:8 NKJV. When we put someone, even our family, before our relationship with God it can hinder our walk with Him. Ask Adam and Eve? It got them and us in a heap of trouble!

Proper spiritual order in our lives is always **God first**, and then spouse, then children, then our vocation, then our church, and then our ministry! Many are the ship wrecked marriages because a father or mother put their children ahead of the spouse and it causes confusion, bitterness and jealousy.

The testimony of many ministers is that they got this confused because of the work load. They had put the ministry and church before their families and they ended up wrecked!

Proper spiritual order is *"Seek first the kingdom of God and His righteousness, and all these things shall be added to you"* Matthew 6:33 NKJV.

Trapped!

Are you trapped like I was?

Well, the grace and love of God is the home plate and only there will you find lasting joy and peace!

The Father is waiting for you to run into His arms! The choice is yours! It is an easy thing to do, so run now and find rest for your soul as you sit in peace with Him! (John 1:12, Luke 15:4-7, Luke

15:20-24, Matthew 11:28-30).

What is the home plate?

The home plate is sitting in the lap of the Father!

It is that deep **understanding** that we are *loved, secure* and *significant* in the secret place with Him. The psalmist summed it up in the 91st Psalm.

> You who sit down in the High God's presence,
> Spend the night in Shaddai's shadow,
> Say this "God is my refuge.
> I trust in you and I'm safe!"
> That's right – He rescues you from hidden traps,
> Shields you from deadly hazards.
> His huge outstretched arms protect you –
> Under them you're perfectly safe;
> His arms fend off all harm.
> Fear nothing – not wild wolfs in the night,
> Not flying arrows in the day,
> Not disease that prowls through the darkness,
> Not disaster that erupts at high noon.
> Even though others succumb all around,
> Drop like flies right and left,
> No harm will even graze you
> You'll stand untouched, watch it all from a distance,
> Watch the wicked turn into corpses.
> Yes, because God's your refuge,
> The High God your very own home,
> Evil can't get close to you,
> Harm can't get through the door.
> He ordered his angels
> To guard you wherever you go.
> If you stumble, they'll catch you;
> Their job is to keep you from falling.

You'll walk unharmed among lions and snakes,
And kick young lions and serpents from the path.
"If you'll hold on to me for dear life," says God
"I'll get you out of trouble.
I'll give you the best of care
If you'll only get to know and trust me.
Call me and I'll answer, be at your side in bad times;
I'll rescue you, then throw you a party.
I'll give you long life,
Give you a long drink of salvation" The Message!

It is the **eternal knowledge** that our Lord Jesus died to demonstrate His redemptive love for us *"in that while we were still sinners Christ died for us"* Romans 5:8 NKJV.

It is the **confidence** that the same Holy Spirit that raised the Lord Jesus from the dead resides in us and will raise our mortal bodies. (Isaiah 25:8, Matthew 27:52, John 6:39, I Corinthians 15:20-21)

It is the **assurance** that He has put all things under His feet and that we participate in the mystery of the final victory! *"Now this I say, brethren that flesh and blood cannot inherit the kingdom of God; nor does corruption inherit incorruption. Behold I tell you a mystery: We shall not all sleep, but we shall all be changed—in a moment, in the twinkling of an eye, at the last trumpet, For the trumpet will sound, and the dead will be raised incorruptible, and we shall be changed. For this corruptible must put on incorruption, and this mortal must put on immortality. So when this corruptible has put on incorruption, and this mortal has put on immortality, then shall be brought to pass the saying that is written:*

Death is swallowed up in victory.
O death, where is thy sting?

O Hades, where is your victory?
The sting of death is sin, and the strength of sin is the law.
But thanks be to God, who gives us the victory through our lord Jesus
Christ. Therefore, my beloved brethren, be steadfast, immovable, always
abounding in the work of the Lord, knowing that your labor is not in
vain in the Lord" I Corinthians 15:50-58 NKJV.

CHAPTER THREE

THE SCIENCE OF FIGHT-OR-FLIGHT

Do you see the beautiful provision that our Father God has given unto us? He has promised us peace, but often we find ourselves thinking, living and walking in the **"resistance stage of fight or flight" (red zone)** and our bodies and minds are rapidly being broken down!

Now that we have seen some of the issues, let's look again at the science of the physical response to stress and anxiety.. I am quoting this from an informative article "The Anatomy of Anxiety" that was in Time Magazine June 10, 2002 written by Alice Park. They quote as their medical source Dr. Dennis S. Charney, M.D. National Institute of Mental Health.

Anxiety and stress what triggers it...?

When the senses pick up a threat – a loud noise, a scary sight, a creepy feeling – the information takes two different routes through the brain.

The shortcut: When startled the brain automatically engages an emergency hot line to its fear center, the amygdala. Once activated, the amygdala sends the equivalent of an all points bulletin that alerts other brain structures. The result is the classic fear response:

41

sweaty palms, rapid heartbeat. Increased blood pressure and a burst of adrenaline. All this happens before the mind is conscious of having smelled or touched anything. Before you know why you're afraid, you are on…. This short cut enables the body to respond to threats even before we become aware of them. We have no control over these responses; it is the way God wired us!

The high road: Only after the fear response is activated does the conscious mind kick into gear. Some sensory information, rather than traveling directly to the amygdala, takes a more circuitous route, stopping first at the thalamus – the processing hub for sensory cues – and then the cortex – the outer layer of the brain cells. The cortex analyzes the raw data streaming in through the senses and decides whether they require a fear response. If they do, the cortex signals the amygdala, and the body stays on alert, causing these responses in the brain.

1- Auditory and visual stimuli:

Sights and sounds are processed, first by the thalamus, which filters the incoming cues and shunts them either directly to the amygdala or to the appropriate parts of the brain.

2- Olfactory and Tactile stimuli:

Smells and touch sensations bypass the Thalamus altogether, taking a short cut directly to the amygdala. Smells, therefore often evoke stronger memories or feelings than do sights and sounds.

3- Thalamus:

The hub for sights and sounds, the thalamus breaks down incoming visual cues by size, shape and color, and auditory cues by volume and dissonance, and then signals the appropriate parts of the cortex.

4- Cortex:

It gives raw sights and sounds meaning, enabling the brain to become conscious of what it is seeing or hearing. One region, the prefrontal cortex, may be vital to turning off the anxiety response once the threat has passed.

5- Amygdala:

The emotional core of the brain, the amygdala has the primary role of triggering the fear response. Information that passes through the amygdala is tagged with emotional significance.

6- Bed nucleus of the stria terminalis:

Unlike the amygdala which sets off an immediate burst of fear, the BNST perpetuates the fear response, causing the longer-term unease typical of anxiety.

7- Locus ceruleus:

It receives the signals from the amygdala and is responsible for initiating many of the classic anxiety responses: rapid heartbeat, increased blood pressure, and sweating and pupil dilation.

8- Hippocampus:

This is the memory center, vital to storing the raw information coming in from the senses, along with the emotional baggage attached to the data during their trip through the amygdala.

How the body responds

It responds by putting the brain on alert; the amygdala triggers a series of changes in the brain chemicals and hormones that puts the entire body in anxiety mode. Here is what is happening as these chemical or hormones travel through the spinal cord to the rest of your body.

1- Stress-Hormone boost:

Responding to the signals from the hypothalamus and pituitary gland, the adrenal glands pump out high levels of the stress hormone cortisol. Too much cortisol short circuits the cells in the hippocampus, making it difficult to organize the memory of a trauma or stressful event. Memories lose their context and become fragmented.

2- Racing Heartbeat:

The body's sympathetic nervous system, responsible for heart rate and breathing, shifts into overdrive. The heart beats faster, blood pressure rises and the lungs hyperventilate. Sweat increases, and even the nerve endings on the skin tingle into action, creating goose bumps.

3- Fight, Flight or Fright:

The senses become hyper alert, drinking in every detail of the surroundings and looking for potential new threats. Adrenaline shoots to the muscles, preparing the body to fight or flee.

4- Digestion Shutdown:

The brain stops thinking about things that bring pleasure, shifting its focus instead to identifying potential dangers. To ensure that no energy is wasted on digestion, the body will sometimes respond by empting the digestive track through involuntary vomiting, urination or defecation.

Real fear

In 1996 I had an experience that absolutely was the most terrifying in my life! As a policeman I had a gun stuck between my eyes and I saw that the man holding the gun was possessed enough to blow my brains out. It didn't happen. Someone described the life of a police office as hours of boredom, interrupted by moments of sheer terror. In my case that fit pretty well; and my son Joe, who was a policeman after graduating from college, had many of the same experiences.

But none of those compared to what I am about to describe. This was a different type of experience that happened with my little girl Lexie when she was three years old.

This is a snake story!

Our family lived in South Georgia on a farm that was sur-
rounded by soybeans, cotton and sorghum fields. We lived on a
three acre track right in the middle of these fields. Then to our west
there were thousands of acres that we leased to a timber company
that grew pine trees.

Lexie and I were in the yard doing some clean up work and taking care of our horse Sweet Jane, an Appaloosa quarter horse.
While in the pasture with the horse I had been trying to teach Lexie
to watch for snakes because we knew that there was abundance of
snakes in the area. We had never seen one, but our neighbors told
us to be cautious.

Lexie went over and got on the swing I had built for her
between two trees, and I was in the dog pen sprucing it up. I
noticed that she had gotten off and could not get herself back on as
she was too small. I went and placed her on the swing, and then
went back to the dog pen which was about 40 feet away. A few
minutes later she hollered at me to help her again. When I looked
in her direction I immediately went into fight-or flight!

There, less than three feet from her, was a six foot long timber
rattlesnake and its head was up looking at her and waving back
and forth. I knew that if she saw it she was capable of trying to pick
it up, because to her it was just a harmless critter.

I immediately started sweating, my heart raced, and without
thinking I ran those forty feet, reached down and grabbed her like
a fumbled football and dove and rolled away from the snake. It
was sort of a dive and roll like I had been trained to do in the
Marine Corps.

People have asked me if I prayed at the time. I do remember
saying, as I was running toward her, "Lord, I can't stand to see that

45

snake bite my little treasure!" But it was not really a prayer, just the plea of a terrified dad. Many of you know it is so different when it is our children.

As I rolled away with Lexie in my arms I kept waiting for that rattlesnake to strike at me. It didn't strike and I ran with Lexie and put her in the dog pen. She was upset about that, but I knew that she would be safe there till I could dispatch the critter and dispatch him I did!

I decided to take the picture of the rattlesnake, because snakes stories are like fish stories and I wanted to have proof of the encounter. I had put on an industrial safety glove to hold the snake since it was oozing something from the head area and I didn't know if it was poison or not. I wanted to be cautious.

Now, look at the picture of me and the rattlesnake and see if you see anything unusual about it.

Do you see it? The glove is on the wrong hand. I am holding the snake with my bare hand. You think I was a little shook up? Yes! And my heart was still beating really fast many hours later. That is fight-or-flight!

Remember, I did not have to instruct my mind and body to react to that danger. God designed me to react that way for my fight-or-flight. In this case it was both fight-and -flight. My body did come back to peace, even though it took a while.

But what if I had continued to think about the danger and the possibilities of that danger? Well, I would have then been in the resistance reaction stage of fight-or-flight and my body instead would be reacting to a perceived danger or remembered danger. The reaction would have been the same as real danger and the damage would continue.

This is where the devil loves to take us. If he can do that then he can slowly break you down. What does the scripture say about fear? *"For God has not given us a spirit of fear, but of power and of love and of a sound mind"* II Timothy 1:7 NKJV.

Obviously we can tell who is responsible for trying to give us fear. The enemy has over 6,000 years of experience of harassing us with fear. He knows that fear will put you in the "red zone" and break down your mind and body. If he can do that to you, then he has captured you and paralyzed you. Many people I meet are in that condition, and sadly most of them don't know it.

Fear is a major "stronghold" and the only real antidote is to trust God. Worry and anxiety are just the "footholds" that, if left unchecked, will soon grow into major "strongholds". A question I often ask people is "are you temporary or eternal?" We say as Christians that we are eternal, but we often act and respond as if this present temporary life is all there is. No, beloved, this life is only the beginning, as we are destined to live eternally, and that is a wonderful thing!

Lord, increase our vision to see who we really are that we can live in peace, knowing that we are eternal!

Are the dots connecting?

When I first saw these realities, I found myself on my face before God thanking Him that I was still alive, for I had lived in the red zone all of my life! I knew that peace, or homeostasis, was an elusive thing for me even as a Christian. Remember that we described the **"resistance reaction"**, well that was me! All of my life was lived in a minor stage of **"fight-or flight"**.

Vivid are the memories of the sudden intense stomach pains that I experienced in military school. They could actually be crippling, and when I was taken to the doctor he told my parents that it was "nerves". That was many years ago. If that had happened to me today they probably would have put me on some tranquilizer. Goodness knows I took enough of my own form of tranquilizers through the years trying to find relief. And I never found it till I was safe in my Father's arms!

CHAPTER FOUR

WHAT WERE THESE TRANQUILIZERS?

*Performing to please people in authority (military school, family & church)

*Performing to excel at athletics (so I would be accepted)

*People pleaser (peer pressure)

*Risk Taker (had to be cool and accepted)

*Fighting (had to constantly prove to myself that I was ok)

*False burden bearing (had to solve everyone's problem)

*Excessive drinking (could wear the mask better)

*Overeating (eat for comfort)

*Ungodly relationships (looking for love in all the wrong places)

*Revengeful and Prideful (had to be right – can't take person al responsibility)

*If-Then syndrome (grass is always greener on the other side)

This is only a short list, but it is indicative of the types of issues that put us in the "red zone".

If the dots are connecting, then you are seeing that there is definite correlation between our relationships with *God, self and others* that can have a direct effect on our bodies and our minds!

As my friend Dr Terry Doan M.D. says *"the body never lies"* Wow! That is a powerful statement. As a surgeon he said that he can cut out the disease, but through many years as a surgeon he has seen too many folks who are so bitter and anxious that he knows their body was put in turmoil (red zone) by these issues, and will continue in turmoil till they deal with the issues. In other words the surgery could be only a temporary fix.

Reid Henson, a dear friend, quotes an African pastor that he knows well and has traveled with as saying *"The body is obedient, it does what it is told"* and that *"Spiritual warfare is a matter of determining who is in control"*. No doubt in my mind that our peace comes only when we are allowing the Holy Spirit to control our lives, and when we lose our peace it is certainly an indication that something else other than the Spirit of God is in control!

David Wilkerson said on September 13, 2004 from the Times Square Church Pulpit Series that *"The Holy Spirit is not fully received until He (the Holy Spirit) is fully in charge. We haven't received Him if we haven't given Him complete control. We have to cast ourselves totally in His care"*

Now, look at my short list of things that come out of my own testimony and let's look a little closer at each and see how the issue brings us into the "red zone".

Performing to please people in authority (military school, family & church)

This is an area that pervades the church and, of course, the world in general. We believe that our happiness and peace will come when we perform, or live up to someone's standard that we perceive they have made for us. Who should we be interested in pleasing? In reality, only the Lord!

Why has this "performance mentality" become so pervasive?

In my case, I grew up in an environment (military school) where the philosophy was the "first runner up was the first loser". So naturally, everyone was trying to be number one, but it does not work that way! Fortunately, my parents were loving folks who always encouraged me to excellence, but reminded me that I was a winner if I gave it my best shot! Looking back I know that the desire of the school was for my good, but they did not understand the principles of spiritual living.

You see, Jesus taught that the greatest among you will be your servant, and Jesus himself lived that out during His walk all the way to the cross. He was always more concerned with others than himself. He said to us: *"You've observed how godless rulers throw their weight around, how quickly a little power goes to their heads. It's not going to be that way with you. Whoever wants to be great must become a servant. Whoever wants to first among you must be your slave. That is what the Son of Man has done: He came to serve, not to be served – and then to give away His life in exchange for the many who are held hostage"* Matthew 20:25-28 The Message.

Being a servant is a whole different concept! I was taught that only the less fortunate and less educated would ever be in a servile role. But you know the exciting thing is that when people get a hold of this servant revelation that they then can be in positions of great authority, influence, and power, and still maintain a servant's heart!

Look at the history of the church and you will see many examples of men and women who were mightily used of God by being the servant to the Lord's body, which is His church, which is His Bride! Beloved, we are called to be servants to the Lord and we do that by serving His body as well as His creation

Performing to excel at athletics (so I would be accepted)
The competition and comparison that we grow up with in

America is horrific! It often begins on the Sunday school and kindergarten playground and continues all the way through school, and then into our adult life. There seems to be no escape. Even from an early age we are often chosen to participate in sport events based on our size, ability, or popularity. In my own case, as a youngster I was picked last to be on the school recess teams, because I was the smallest boy in my class.

So this begins a process of comparison to other people, and when you compare yourself to others you rarely like the results. This ungodly comparison will quickly result in bitterness toward yourself, or self hatred.

Remember Susie? Well, her testimony was that after Johnny took another girl to the dance that she never felt like she was special. In fact, she said that "she felt very unlovely"

Ungodly competition is also a sure recipe for developing bitterness toward those you are competing with. Many say, what's wrong with competition? Nothing, absolutely nothing, as long as you can compete and still maintain your peace! If you can go play a game of golf and lose without losing your peace then you are probably ok. But, if when you lose you can't sleep at night waiting for another chance to get even, then it has become ungodly! Comparison and competition are open doorways for a "spirit of jealousy" to find a foothold in you life. That "spirit of jealousy" can quickly lead to far more serious issues, even murder!

I highly recommend Dr. Bonnie Chavda's book *"The Original Sin"* published by Destiny Image Publishers, Inc. Shippensburg, Pa. She portrays a powerful vignette of Cain and Abel that describes in a riveting manner how jealousy destroys! It makes the bible story come alive and demonstrates how destructive competition and comparison are.

Paul said to the Corinthian church: *"We do not dare to classify or compare ourselves with some who commend themselves. When they meas-*

ure themselves by themselves and compare themselves with themselves, they are not wise" II Corinthians 10:12 NIV.

A pastor friend of mine who was the administrator of a large Christian school made this observation in 28 years of teaching Christian kids. He said "that 90% of first graders feel good about themselves, but that 80% of fifth graders feel bad about themselves! In the opinion of this administrator, the reason for the change was due to competition and comparison among the children.

Even though they tried to prevent it, he witnessed many examples of the teachers even pitting one child against another. Usually with statements like "If you want to be as smart as little Johnny then you will have to make better grades. Johnny will grow up and make a lot of money and you will just be cleaning the gutters." This entire drama taking place in a Christian school! That would be almost unbelievable if we didn't have the revelation of the spiritual warfare that is being waged against our children!

People Pleaser (so I would be accepted)

Here comes that fabricated personality! We often will do or say anything to be a part of the crowd and that includes doing and saying things that are against our better judgment. But the need to feel secure and significant can be overwhelming, particularly as a young person. The problem is that when we are living a lie that at some point it is no longer a lie and a familiar spirit has gained not just a foothold, but a stronghold!

Risk Taker (had to be cool and accepted)

Thinking about some of the things that I did when I was younger, and some when I was not so much younger literally almost make me break out in a sweat. But you know what? It was more important to be cool and accepted than worry about the dan-

53

ger.

My sweet wife Tonda, in her desire to be accepted as a teenager ended up in the company of the "Hell's Angels" motorcycle gang! She never felt like she fit in, so in her need to be accepted, safe, secure and significant; she started hanging out with people that would accept her. The risks involved were not as important as being cool and accepted.

Praise God, He delivered her from that before the enemy could destroy her, and God set her on a path of real life and ministry! She is a wonderful wife, help mate and mother to our daughters, Taylor and Lexie. In fact, when I need ministry I go to her first!

When you are secure in your position in Christ, then every joy and thrill will come by just being in His presence! You will not need any thing else. As the saying goes "there is no high like Jesus"!

Fighting (had to constantly prove to myself that I was ok)

Remember me telling you that I was often the last one picked on the recess playground? Well, I figured out at an early age that I might be small, but I could be tough! That seemed to impress people. I think that it has been called the Napoleon complex. That developed into a mean streak that was definitely ungodly and very dangerous, almost getting me killed on a couple of occasions.

Now my only desire is to be a warrior for the Lord, and those battles are really exciting!

The words of the Lord are true: *"Not by might nor by power, but by my Spirit, says the Lord of hosts"* Zechariah 4:6 NKJV.

False Burden Bearing (had to solve everyone else's problem)

This is a very subtle area and hard to recognize, because there is a fine line between a real burden and a false burden.

Usually with a real burden you will expend ɣ ceding for the person or situation, rather than just ta. rying about it.

What do we mean by false bearding bearing? A good definitᵤ is "seeing a problem in someone else and you being the one that has to fix it" This can happen with our friends, fellow workers, neighbors, church members, and especially our family members.

Some say "You mean I am not supposed to be concerned about my children and other family members?" No! That is not what we are saying!

Each of us usually has very real concerns for people and family members, but realistically there is only so much you can do about it. But your Father God can do all things about it! He created them, and His love for them is far greater than our love! We often need to release them into His hands to have His way in their lives. His ways are higher than our ways, and He is certainly capable of handling any situation.

It becomes false burden bearing when we decide that only we have the answer and the solution for the person or the problem! In other words, we believe that we are the only one that can fix it! We have to be the "fix it" person!

If you are concerned about your children or someone else you love, then go to them in love and in the spirit of grace and share your concerns. But once you have done that, leave it and them alone, and then pour out your heart to the Father that He will have His way!

Staying in someone's face about their situation is like the proverb which says: *"He who passes by and meddles in a quarrel not his own is like one who takes a dog by the ears"* Proverbs 26:17 NKJV.

There is a scriptural principle that when a man marries that *"he shall leave his father and mother and be joined (cleave) to his wife"* (Genesis 2:24). Many people ignore this admonition and insist on trying to run their children's lives. A minister friend of mine had one son who had recently married and was living near his family. The new wife was home sick, far from home, and on top of that things were rocky in their new married relationship. During a tense and unpleasant argument the new bride locked herself in the bedroom and refused to come out. The son, not knowing what to do, called his father and mother for help! Big mistake!

At that point, Dad and Mom should have offered some advice and stayed out of it, but no, they came right over to the son's house to handle the problem. Another big mistake! The dad falsely thought that he was "Mr. fix it".

The father told me that "I went to the bedroom door and demanded that she come out as she was acting like a brat, and that she had no right to treat his son with such disrespect".

Well, at that point the dad was *taking the new wife by the ears*, and an earful was what he got. She opened the door all right and read him the riot act in language that is unprintable.

Sadly, the father in-law never understood what had happened with his son's wife, and their relationship was continually strained after that. In fact, the young couple eventually moved to another state.

You see the father was moving in areas where he had no authority, and that created a breach that only got worse over time. It also opened the door for a spirit of rejection, as this young bride felt totally alone. Remember, the girl was already homesick and not feeling secure in the new marriage and now the father in-law pours gas on the already burning fire. He would have been fine to offer his son some counsel and then back off, but he violated the principle that a "man shall leave his father and mother and be joined (cleave) to his wife". When that happened the enemy got a "Foothold" in the daughter in-law that became a "Stronghold", because the father never repented for his actions.

We have counseled with many people through the years who have been estranged from their loved ones because of false burden bearing, or of taking on a responsibility that is not theirs.

Saints, the *"government is on His shoulders"* Isaiah 9:6 KJV, not ours! To take His government on our shoulders will certainly cause us to break down and you will be in the "red zone" with all of the negative, tormenting things going on in your mind and body. Would you not agree? Let God be God! He alone can truly handle it!!

There is a wonderful book by Dutch Sheets on praying for your family called "Watchman Prayer" published by Regal Books, Ventura, California. I would recommend it for those struggling with members of your family.

Excessive Drinking (could wear the mask better)

It has been said, and I would agree, that all addictions stem from not liking ourselves!

Why do we do it? Just to cover up the pain, as it is easier to convince yourself that you are ok when your mind is passive from too much alcohol. Also, familiar spirits will find a home in the passive mind.

It is a widely accepted statistic that 4 out of 10 of high school girls drink alcohol, compared to 5 out of 10 of boys. Interestingly enough girls outpace boys in the use of prescription drugs. The reason is probably because prescription drugs are easier to ingest than, say, alcoholic beverages. Guys will often experiment with cigarettes, alcohol and drugs in a search for thrills or to fit in with a crowd, while girls are motivated by a desire to reduce stress or alleviate depression. Girls are more likely to abuse substances if they reached puberty early, had eating disorders, or were physically or sexually abused. However, the desire to be accepted as part of the group is always very strong.

Remember, we all have a need to be loved, feel secure, and be significant! Tragically, none of these false comforters, or face masks, will solve the problem. In fact, addictions only make them worse, causing untold torment in our lives and the lives of those around us. I don't know that I have ever met a family that did not have at least one of the family members struggling with addictions. If you doubt this, just consider the over 20,000 people killed each year in the United States by drinking or impaired drivers. The financial and emotional cost is staggering!

We are a nation that, in many ways, is spiraling out of control as we are losing more and more of our youth to the enemy's tactics! Look around church. The evidence is staggering! And it is an indictment on the Christian community that we have not revealed the love and dynamic life that is ours through Christ. I am encouraged to know many young people who have given their life to walk with the Lord. They are such a testimony to His love and grace.

I know growing up it seemed to be a common practice for folks to do what they wanted to on Saturday night as long as they were in church on Sunday morning. I was no exception, and have repented for not being a true testimony.

Our children desire a supernatural life. God designed us to live that way, but they will only see it as they see it in the adults who are the examples. We need the power of God to fall on our young people, but fruitfulness only comes out of intimacy with the Lord, and it has to start with us!

Overeating (eating for comfort)

This is another form of addiction, and many of the issues and problems are the same.

Obesity: A looming national threat! Just today that was a headline on a web page dedicated to health issues. Not a week goes by that the media is not focusing on the ever growing problem of obesity in America. It is an issue that the church does not like to tackle, because we don't want to embarrass or offend anyone, and it has become so commonplace that often we don't even think about it.

That does not alter the facts that the "Centers for Disease Control and Prevention" estimate that 2 of 3 American adults and 1 of 6 of adolescents are considered overweight or obese. The percentage of adults who are obese – defined as having a body mass index of 30 or more has doubled to an alarming 60 million people. Some statistics show the figures much higher. Those are sobering statistics and should get our attention. The "National Institute of Health" has suggested that our life expectancy is dropping by 5 years due to this problem.

Food or Junk?

My friend and medical counselor, Dr. Franklin H. Ross, Jr., taught me an important concept regarding food and why so many people are sick and dying. He said "Ish, there is no such thing as junk food! It is either food or it is junk"! Wow, that sure helped me to change the way I was looking at food, and to understand what the food was doing to my body. The truth is as he explained what we eat is either food that is nutritious and sustains life, or it is junk which becomes toxic or death in our bodies!

He also reminded me of the scripture in Corinthians regarding our bodies being the temple of the Holy Spirit. It says *"Do you not know that you are the temple of God and that the Spirit of God dwells in you? If anyone defiles (destroys) the temple of God, God will destroy him.*

For the temple of God is holy, which temple you are" I Corinthians 3:16-17 NKJV.

We have a spiritual responsibility to our Lord to take care of the temple (body) that He has given us for His glory. He has promised to hold us accountable!

Remember Paul's words *"I beseech you therefore brethren, by the mercies of God, that you present your bodies a living sacrifice, holy, acceptable to God, which is your reasonable service"* Romans 12:1NKJV.

Who can deny that food tastes great? The problem is that we eat for comfort! We have a hard day, a fuss with someone, or are just generally stressed out and we fly to the cabinet or the fridge to find that solace that is there in the ice cream or cake. I know I speak from experience.

Then, there is the programming that we often grow up with, that food is a source of pleasure and comfort. You remember those times as a child when you came in from a hard day at school and mother said "here have a piece of my favorite chocolate cake it will make you feel better". And you know what? That piece of cake did make you feel better, but it may have also started you on a path of eating for comfort!

Oh, and there is the church that loves to enjoy the fellowship of each other, and often the fellowship is centered on food. How many functions have we been to where the food was just delicious? From an early age we are trained or conditioned that food is always a part of fellowship. Not just at church, but PTA meetings, social and civic clubs, business meetings and family gatherings. For me the treat of going to my great aunt Gigi's house for Christmas was the knowledge that she had made her special home made fudge! Now many years later, I still have fond memories about that fudge! In fact, my mouth can start watering just thinking about the special fudge and I have not had any for many years. That is classical conditioning!

This can also be called the conditioned response, and the first known research was done by Ivan P. Pavlov 1849-1936. A Russian physiologist whose interest in conditioning launched him on a 35 year study resulting in a series of famous lectures that were published in 1927. His work was so well known and respected that he won a Nobel Prize for medicine in 1904.

This famous work showed and proved that dogs can be conditioned to salivate for food even when the food is not present. How did he do this? He did it by conditioning the dog to associate the ringing of a bell with food. After some time he would remove the food, but still ring the bell. The previous conditioning of the bell and food together would still provoke the response, even when there was no food present! The bell alone would provoke the salivating response, because now the dog associated the bell with the food.

We all have bells that bring about certain responses in our minds and bodies, because we have been conditioned by our experiences and our expectations. This is very important in ministry and reinforces the need to have our minds renewed!

If food rings your bell, then ask the Father to change the bell!

Jesus said these powerful words: *"I am the bread of life. Your fathers ate manna in the wilderness, and they died. This is the bread which comes down out of heaven, so that one may eat of it and not die. I am the living bread that came down out of heaven; if anyone eats of this bread, he shall live for ever; and the bread also which I shall give for the life of the world is my flesh"* John 6:48-51 NAS.

Beloved, Jesus is offering us real bread that does not spoil, but gives eternal life to all who eat it. Total is the comfort we receive from the one who will never leave us or forsake us, and that can never be replaced by chocolate cake!

Ungodly relationship (looking for love in all the wrong places)

This is a very evil and devastating trap that most people have fallen into at one time or another in their life. The "why" that people get involved in ungodly (not God honoring) relationships is simple. We all have three basic needs:

1- Feel loved
2- Feel secure
3- Feel significant

If we don't feel loved, secure or significant in our homes, churches, school, etc. we will find a place or people that will fulfill our needs! Guaranteed! All too often, we find that love, security, or significance in a bottle, pills, and illicit lover's arms. And often all of these run together!

This was the story of the woman at the well in John chapter 4. This dear woman had been married 5 times and was now living with a 6th man when she had the encounter with Jesus, the living water. That encounter changed her life and set her free from all of her past sins and challenges, not to mention that she became the first woman evangelist in the New Testament!

Our gal had spent her life looking and longing for that which no man could ever fill! And many of us have done the same thing, and all to no avail. All of these encounters had only built strongholds of shame, guilt, bitterness, self bitterness and a long line of unfulfilled expectations and broken dreams.

The beautiful thing about this story is that the woman was delivered by an encounter with the living God! Her past became her past, and after being touched by the master she became whole and new. She did not have to go through months or years of counseling and ministry to be free! She only had to meet the one called

Wonderful, Counselor, Mighty God, Everlasting Father, Prince of Peace! His name was Jesus!

She did not just know about Jesus – No, she met Him and He touched her!

She received "the Master's Touch"!

That is the goal of ministry! To introduce creation to the One called *Wonderful, Counselor, Mighty God, Everlasting Father and Prince of Peace!* Yes! You want your mind and body to be in peace? Then release yourself to the *Prince of Peace*, who alone can fulfill you!

Don't put God in a box as to how He can minister to you!

This ministry of restoration can be accomplished in many scriptural ways.

1- Teaching and Exhortations
2- Prayer for healing
3- Revelation and Counseling
4- Deliverance
5- Signs and wonders
6- Miracles
7- Impartation of the Spirit and Life

The dear woman at the well was ministered to in all these ways, yet the process took only a conversation to impart the Spirit and Life as she was taught where her deliverance was coming from and Who her healer was! She was immediately (word of knowledge) brought to the place where she became a seeker of the truth and no longer just wanted to hear about the Messiah. No! She now wanted to follow Him! She was tired of being thirsty (need to be loved, need to be secure and the need to be significant) She had now found the Messiah who alone could give her living water. He alone had the words of Life and she wanted that life!

The footholds that had become strongholds in her life were cast down and shattered in one meeting!

Revengeful and Prideful (had to be right – can't take personal responsibility)

The longer I live, and the longer I am in ministry, the more I am overwhelmed by the tormenting and devastating issue of pride!

I recently did an unscientific study of men who were successful, but were at the same time miserable failures with their fellow laborers and their families. Some of these men were in the ministry, while some of them were professionals and others were craftsmen. All of these fellows were very skilled in their profession and had been successful, at least to a measure. Yet despite that, there was a testimony of bad and broken relationships around those people that had worked closely with them. Those problems with relationships and relational attitudes had also spread into their respective families. There was a long line of wounded people that was in the wake of their critical attitude, condemnation, demeaning words and actions, arrogance, anger and defilement!

How could this be present in men of deep spiritual understanding and stature?

Simple! As I studied these folks over a period of time I came to the conclusion that the one thing they all in common was PRIDE!

Pride is a destroyer. It will destroy you and it will destroy those around you.

Pride is really just being determined to run our own lives and not let God have His rightful place. We have all been guilty! But, you cannot just repent for pride as you could for, say, the sin of adultery or slander. **No, the only solution to pride is to humble yourself!**

Both James and Peter say: *"God resists the proud, but gives* **grace** *to the **humble***" James 4:6, I Peter 5:5 NKJV.

When you are moving in pride you have placed yourself in an adversarial position with God!

*"For by **grace** you have been saved through faith, and that not of yourself; it is a gift of God"* Ephesians 2:8 NKJV.

Did you save yourself? No! He saved you through the giving of His own blood.

Well, if He can save you through you're yielding (humble) to His kingdom, then don't you think it is reasonable to believe that He is capable of running your life as you also yield (humble) to Him on a daily basis?

Pride produces revenge, because pride can never own up to issues. It is always someone else's fault! It is similar to the dynamic that I saw in prison ministry. I very rarely talked to a guilty man or woman. It was always the other person's fault! We are a society infected with the inability to accept responsibility. But until we do we will have a hard time getting healed and being a vessel of honor. There are whole segments of our society that are plagued with a victim mentality. It fact, the victim mentality has become their identity!

A recent event in Charlotte, N.C. underscores this mentality and the way it has become a generational curse for many in our society.

A young boy of 13 stole a car and took it on what he called a "joyride". He also had a number of other young teenagers in the car with him when they crashed into a young mother and her infant child. The infant was not harmed, but the mother suffered severe injuries that will stay with her for life.

The mother of the teenager who stole the car and wrecked it was interviewed on television and was quoted as saying that "it was not her child's fault, but rather society's fault as her child was deprived of a lot of basic pleasures since they were on a limited income".

The highway patrol charged the teenager with a variety of charges, ranging from stealing the car to driving recklessly. They estimated his speed at over 70 mph in a 35 mph zone on a curvy road. The story got even weirder when the mother of the teenager blamed the wreck on the steering and brakes on the stolen car as being defective. Therefore, her child was not at fault and she was considering suing the car manufacturer! This is a true story, and if it were not so sad it would make a good comedy.

A lady in town wrote the newspaper this letter entitled "Woman injured in crash with stolen car full of teenagers" She said "Now whenever anyone asks her what's wrong with our society? I can just pull out a copy of this story and show them all the quotes by this mother making all the excuses for her rebellious and criminal teenage son." She said that this mother is the perfect spokeswoman – by word and example – to never, ever accept personal responsibility. The writer said "that no amount of money, perks, better schools, or federal mandate can ever compensate for that depth of ignorance and deficiency of conscience!"

How many children grow up in that deficiency of conscience? The truth is that number is in the multiple millions!

Any person who lives in the *"I will"* realm will never be truly useful in the kingdom of God. Lay down the spirit of Lucifer which proclaimed *"I will ascend"* Isaiah 14:12-15 NKJV

And take up the spirit of the living Christ which is a servant!

The "Limp"

Years of ministry has taught me some hard lessons about getting under the covering umbrella of certain men. My counsel to folks now is to see if that man or woman's ministry walks with a limp. If no limp, don't connect with them as you will sooner or

66

later end up being defiled by their arrogance and pride.

Peter had to first be sifted before he could be a useful servant! (Luke 22:31-34) Before he was sifted he was moving in the "I will" realm and he would have been dangerous if he had not been sifted! The "I will" realm is also called "pride"!

Deanne Day has an excellent book titled *"Sifted Like Wheat-Turning Pride into Promotion through Repentance"* that is available through Restoring Hearts International, P.O. Box 3016, Murrells Inlet, SC 29576. She treats this subject of sifting very thoroughly and with great insight into the causes of siftings.

Some people are blaming the enemy or circumstances, when actually they may be in a sifting process!

Being under the umbrella of a man who has no limp is like trying to ride an unbroken wild stallion. You see a horse that has not been broken is very satisfied in his own little kingdom. The horse has not learned to serve and until he does learn to serve he will be very dangerous. He is living in the "I want - what I want - when I want it" realm. Sort of like a spoiled child that has never been under discipline. It has taken me a couple of serious mistakes over the years to sort this out, but now I know how to look for the limp! These mistakes were not only damaging to me, but also damaging to my family.

Jacob went through a "sifting" that brought him to the place of a name change, because he had a change in his nature! He was finally lining up with God's way of thinking! The limp is detailed in the story of Jacob's wrestling with God in Genesis 32:22-32. The limp is the evidence of a man or woman that has been broken and can now be a servant of God! **God's kingdom has become more important than their personal kingdom.** If this work has not been done, then they will surely be more than a thorn in your side. It is not a matter of "if" you will be defiled and wounded; it is only a matter of "when" it will happen!

Many dear believers have been wounded by prideful, religious, unsanctified hirelings. Those wounds have caused a spirit of betrayal along with a broken heart to now be a part of their identity. Subsequently, they find it difficult to trust God or God's real servants, and they are living in a place of unrest.

What does unrest do to your mind and body? It puts you in the "red zone'!

Beloved, our God is looking for those who are willing to lay down their lives for the sheep! Will you be one of those?

If-Then syndrome (the grass is always greener on the other side)

The writer to the Hebrews made a powerful statement when he said:

"Don't be obsessed with getting material things. Be relaxed with what you have. Since God assured us, "I'll never let you down. Never walk off and leave you," we can boldly quote, "God is there, ready to help; I'm fearless no matter what. Who or what can get to me?"
Hebrews 13:5-6 The Message.

Contentment, or the rather the lack of contentment, is definitely a "red zone" stressor. How many times have you heard someone say "If only I had a different job, had more money, was better looking, had a different spouse, had a spouse, or didn't have a spouse, had a bigger house, had a different car...... and the list goes on! All of these issues will put you into a stress situation where your adrenaline and cortisol are working overtime and that is compromising your immune system by destroying your B cells and T cells.

My dear friend George Thrash taught me the principle that the "grass always looks greener on the other side, but you still have to cut it"! He tells a story of a man he was ministering to on a lay renewal that had left his wife of many years for a much younger woman. It was only after they were married a short while that the man realized that his new wife was very demanding and selfish, not to mention some more serious issues. He knew that he had made a horrible mistake, and he told George "The grass sure looked greener, but I figured out too late that you still have to cut it". Do you get it? The grass may look better, taste better, feel better, be more expensive, etc., but you still have to cut it! He learned this principle while ministering to many people that were always looking for the "better" thing, thinking that would make them happy, but of course it never did!

Ephesians 2:14a says *"For He is our peace"*. Beloved we need no other. So many folks hate where they are in present circumstances, but our circumstances are not what should define our joy. Our joy is in the Father, Son and Holy Spirit.

If we want true joy then our desire must be that of the psalmist when he said: *"You will show me the path of life;* **In your presence is fullness of joy;** *At your right hand are* **pleasures forevermore***"* Psalm 16: NKJV.

Oswald Chambers made a classic statement when asked how he gets so much done on a daily basis as only one man. He replied that **"It's easy, I have faith, and do the next thing!"** His peace was in the fact the Father was watching over him and that he could only do as much as he could do. So he just rejoiced in every moment!

As my wife Tonda likes to say "he had learned to enjoy the dance"!

That peace is ours church, Take it!

Chapter Five

Answer to tranquilizers is Repentance!

The answer has been missed many times because it is so simple! We often want a complicated regimen or formula that will work, but that is usually just another form of performance or works.

No, the gospel is simple and God designed it to be simple. Otherwise, only the very bright would be able to grasp it. The Lord Jesus used simple men to teach and minister in His kingdom, and He only asks for a simple response!

The scriptures clearly teach this simple truth from Genesis to Revelation! The truth is that the door to salvation and life is REPENTANCE. Now we know that Jesus is the door, but REPENTANCE is what opens the door!

Is that too simple? No! Jesus said: *"And you shall know the truth, and the truth shall make you free"* John 8:32 NAS.

Before Jesus came on the scene, John the Baptist came, and what did he teach? Repentance!

Matthew chapter three says: *"Now in those days John the Baptist came preaching in the wilderness of Judea saying, "Repent, for the kingdom of heaven is at hand."*

For this is the one referred to Isaiah the prophet, saying. "The voice of one crying in the Wilderness, Make ready the way of the Lord, Make His paths straight!"

Now John himself had a garment of camel's hair, and a leather belt about his waist; his food was locusts and wild honey.

Then Jerusalem was going out to him, and all Judea, and all the district around the Jordan;

And they were being baptized by him in the Jordan River, as they confessed their sins.

But when he saw many of the Pharisees and Sadducees coming for baptism, he said to them "You brood of vipers, who warned you to flee from the wrath to come?

Therefore bring forth fruit in keeping with your **repentance***;"*

"And do not suppose that you can say to yourselves, we have Abraham for our father; for I say to you, that God is able from these stones to raise up children to Abraham.

And the axe is already laid at the root of the trees; every tree therefore that does not bear good fruit is cut down, and thrown into the fire.

And His winnowing fork is in His hand, and He will thoroughly clean His threshing-floor; and He will gather His wheat into the barn, but He will burn up the chaff with unquenchable fire"

Then Jesus arrived from Galilee at the Jordan coming to John, to be baptized by him.

But John tried to prevent Him saying, "I have need to be baptized by you, and do you come to me?"

But Jesus answering said to him, "Permit it at this time; for in this way it is fitting for us to fulfill all righteousness." Then he permitted Him.

And after being baptized, Jesus went up immediately from the water; and behold, the heavens were opened, and he saw the Spirit of God descending as a dove, and coming upon Him;

And behold a voice out of the heavens, saying, "This is My beloved Son, in whom I am well pleased" Matthew 3:1-17 NAS.

John got it all started as a forerunner, but Jesus and the other disciples He called continued the teaching of **repentance**!

When you study the gospels and the life of Jesus you will find that He basically taught and did five things.

1- He taught repentance
2- He healed the sick
3- He cast out demons
4- He worked many miracles
5- He did many signs and wonders

What is repentance? According to Webster's Dictionary it is "to change ones mind concerning past actions". Yes, I believe that is true, but it also has to change the further actions of the person, or it is not really repentance.

Many are going to be the lost and desperate people who were told that all they had to do to have a born again experience was come to an altar and say, or make a confession, that they were taking Jesus as their salvation. Well that is a nice start, but if they have not been taught that they have a need to repent, then they will not have a changed life which is the evidence of true repentance and salvation! Jesus made it clear that we have to repent, or line up our thinking with God's thinking in order to come into His kingdom. It must be considered a spurious conversion if there is no true repentance. There are no shortcuts!

In Matthew's gospel quoted above we hear John the Baptist say some harsh words to the religious (Pharisees & Sadducees) people that wanted to be baptized. He said to them *"You brood of vipers, who warned you to flee and escape from the wrath and indignation (of God against disobedience) that is coming?* **Bring forth fruit that is consistent with repentance – let your lives prove your change of heart"** Matthew 3:7-8 AMP.

I remember well, during a ministry session, a man telling me that his adultery was not a problem, because he had been to the altar and was born again. Beloved, that is the ultimate deception. God hates sin and when we are converted we will hate it too. The lack of proper teaching and the lack of repentance is the reason that 80% of the people that claim to have had a born again experience fall away from the faith. That figure is staggering, but true!

Charles G. Finney, in the classic "True and False Repentance" published by Kregel Publications, Grand Rapids, Michigan, copyright 1966, goes to great depth in challenging our ideas and perceptions about what repentance is and why true repentance is necessary for salvation.

He makes a clear distinction between sorrow and repentance, and uses as a scriptural basis II Corinthians 7:10. *"For the sorrow that is according to the will of God produces repentance without regret, leading to salvation; but the sorrow of the world produces death"* KJV.

Mr. Finney says "Suppose a person admits in theory that sin deserves eternal death. He does not believe it or it would be impossible for him to remain a careless sinner. A person may see sin to be hurtful and abominable, while yet his heart loves it, and desires it, and clings to it. But when he truly repents, he most heartily abhors and renounces it."

"In relation to God, he feels toward sin as it really is. And here is the source of those gushings sorrow in which Christians sometimes break out, when contemplating sin. The Christian views it as to its nature and simply feels abhorrence. But when he views it in relation to God, then he weeps; the fountains of sorrow gush forth, and he wants to get right down on his face and pour out a flood of tears over his sins."

Casual Sin = Casual Repentance!

I think that we would all agree that even the church's attitude toward sin has become very casual! And if our attitude toward sin is casual then it stands to reason that our attitude toward repentance is also casual!

I like to call it the bikini principle! I remember as a child that when we would go to the beach that it was common knowledge that any woman who would wear a string bikini was a "morally loose woman". Wow, how times have changed. Now it is almost impossible to even buy an attractive one piece swimsuit.

Ok, you don't like that example. How about the fact that we have taken prayer out of schools, abortion is available almost everywhere, sexual abuse is rampant in our churches and families, homosexuality, adultery and perversion is winked at even in many of our churches. Gossip, slander and disrespect as become commonplace in almost every area of society! Yes, dear ones, we have become too casual!

You see what happens on this slippery slope? If we have become casual about sin, then of course we have also become casual about repentance. Why? Because if sin is not a big issue then repentance is not a big issue either!

Beloved, these are not casual observations, these are hard facts!

Praise God! He is moving and drawing His people to a fresh understanding of sin and repentance, and it is part of His plan as He prepares His bride to meet the bridegroom. She (the church) will be without spot or wrinkle, but the wedding will not take place till there is a deeper and clearer understanding of repentance!

Definition of Repentance!

My definition of repentance is simply: **"bringing our thinking in line with God's truth, or to bring our thinking into line with the way God thinks."**

For me that keeps it simple! Just line up with God's thinking!

Can we know how God thinks? Yes! How do we know how God thinks? By knowing His word!

We have to know His word, which is the express nature of who God is! We have to have an intimate relationship with the son, the Lord Jesus, because the son is the *"image of the invisible God"* Colossians 1:15 NKJV, and *"He (Jesus) is the radiance of His glory and exact representation of His nature"* Hebrews 1:3 NKJV. We know that *"faith comes by hearing and hearing by the word of God"* Romans 10:17 NKJV. It is clear that we must *"study to show ourselves approved unto God"* II Timothy 2:15 NKJV.

If we are acting, thinking, speaking or in any way being contrary to the nature of God then we need to repent! It is just that simple!

Lord's Prayer

For example, the word says in the Lord's Prayer: *"And forgive us our debts, as we have forgiven our debtors."* Matthew 6:12 NAS. So, if we are harboring unforgiveness toward someone, then we are contrary to the nature of God, and we need to repent. That is pretty simple.

Hating our brother

If we find ourselves in the place of hating our brother, then we are contrary to the nature of God which says: *"He who says he is in the light, and hates his brother, is in darkness until now"* I John 2:9 NKJV. and *"Whoever does not practice righteousness is not of God, nor is he who does not love his brother"* I John 3:10 NKJV; then we need to repent and get our thinking and actions lined up with God.

Rejoicing

If we find that we are not *"Rejoicing evermore, praying without ceasing and in all things giving thanks; for this is the will of God in Christ Jesus for you"* I Thessalonians 5:16-18 NKJV, then we need to repent and move into the will (thinking) of God!

Knowing His word, you know that there is a curse for not rejoicing in God and serving Him with joy and gladness, for He said: *"Moreover all these curses shall come upon you and pursue and overtake you, until you are destroyed, because you did not obey the voice of the Lord your God to keep His commandments and His statutes which He commanded you. And they shall be upon you for a sign and a wonder, and on your descendants forever. Because you did not serve the Lord your God with joy and gladness of heart, for the abundance of everything"* Deuteronomy 28:47 NKJV.

Tithing

Often overlooked is the principle of tithing which is clearly defined in scripture. Pastors are sometimes hesitant to teach the principle of tithing, because they are afraid the sheep will be offended. That needs to change, because there is a curse associated with the lack of tithing and the ministry has a solemn responsibility to teach the principle.

Let's look at the scripture from Malachi that is very clear – words are not vague at all regarding the outcome of neglecting the tithe! If we neglect the tithe we are actually inviting a curse of the marauders and plunderers.

"I am God—yes, I Am. I haven't changed. And because I haven't changed, you, the descendants of Jacob, haven't been destroyed. You have a long history of ignoring my commands. You haven't done a thing I've told you. Return to me so I can return to you," says GOD-of-the-

Angel-Armies. You ask, 'But how do we return?' Begin by being honest. Do honest people rob God? But you rob me day after day." You ask, 'How have we robbed you?' The tithe and the offering—that's how! **And now you're under a curse**—*the whole lot of you—because you're robbing me. Bring your full tithe to the Temple treasury so there will be ample provisions in my Temple. Test me in this and see if I don't open up heaven itself to you and pour out blessings beyond your wildest dreams. For my part, I will defend you against marauders; protect your wheat fields and vegetable gardens against plunderers." You'll be voted "Happiest Nation." You'll experience what it's like to be a country of grace." God-of-the-Angel-Armies says so"* Malachi 3:6-12 The Message.

This is a powerful scripture that is often overlooked and ignored. Many are the Christians under the *marauders and plunderers* power because they have ignored God and His clear mandate!

The remedy is simple. **Repent and be obedient.** Line up your thinking with God's thinking and watch the heavens open up for you and your family.

Some say "I just don't have enough money!" Well, test God as He says to do and let Him prove that He is faithful. I did years ago and God has never let me down, and I have been through some tough and tight places!

What is faith?

Let me give you a definition of faith that may help you walk through some of these tough issues and principles that I learned from Dr. James B. Richards. **"Faith is simply a response to God's character. It is the natural response for someone who believes God is honest! Unbelief is also a response to God's character – it does not believe that God is honest"**

78

Ok, now the choice is up to you. Are you going to believe that God is honest, or is He just pulling your leg? God is honest and He wants you to know that He is honest and loves you. Try Him, test Him, *He says Try me now in this, if I will not open the windows of heaven and pour out for you such blessing that there will not be room enough to receive it"* Malachi 3:10 NKJV.

Another definition of faith would be for you **"to get in step with what God has already said."** For instance, in this tithing issue, to get in step would be to just do it! Do what? Tithe!

Jesus said in Mark 16:15-18 *"Go into all the world and preach the gospel to every creature. He who believes and is baptized will be saved, but he who does not believe will be condemned. And these signs will follow those who believe: In my name they will cast out demons; they will speak with new tongues; they will take up serpents; and if they drink anything deadly, it will by no means hurt them; they shall lay hands on the sick, and they will recover"* NKJV.

So to be in step with the word of God we would do it!

Again Jesus said some powerful words that often get overlooked when he said: *"Truly, truly, I say to you, he who* **believes** *in Me, the works that I do shall he do also; and greater works shall he do; because I go to the Father"* John 14:12 NAS.

Now, what would those works be that Jesus is referring to?

1- He taught repentance
2- He healed the sick
3- He cast out demons
4- He worked many miracles
5- He did signs and wonders

Now, to believe in Him would mean not just intellectually, but experientially! How do you do that? By your actions! You believe His word and you step out in faith and trust God for the outcome.

I personally never saw anyone healed until I stepped out and started praying for people. When I was obedient and started praying for people I started seeing people getting healed. And so will you, because that is getting in step with what God has already ordained for "believers"!

Are you a believer? If so, step out and see if God is honest!

Trusting your own understanding?

Proverbs 3:5-8 says *"Trust in the Lord with all your heart, and lean not on your own understanding; In all your ways acknowledge Him, and He shall direct your paths. Do not be wise in your own eyes; fear the Lord and depart from evil. It will be health to your body (navel) and strength to your bones"* NKJV.

We have been so programmed to believe that our intellect is all we need, that we spend countless hours and years refining a tool (brain) that God gave us, but all too often without acknowledging Him!

Am I against education and further learning? No! Absolutely not! It has been proven that as we continue to develop our mind that issues like dementia will rarely touch us. We have to exercise those precious resources that God gifted us with, or we will lose them. The parable of the talents illustrates this well. (Matthew 25:14-30) If you don't use what you have been given to make it fruitful and increase then you will probably lose the little bit you started out with. God never called us to be mediocre. He calls us to be the best!

How do you acknowledge Him? By talking to Him and listening to Him. It is just that simple, but it does require time and effort. Is it unreasonable to spend time and listen to the Father of life who has created you, redeemed you, delivered you from darkness, and only wants the very best for you? How will you know His plans for your life if you don't know Him and spend time with Him? You won't, and that is where we get in trouble!

Someone said it like this. We have no right to "self determination"! Even if you look at it logically, you have to agree that if God made us, then He has a plan for us and true joy will only be ours when His plan is worked out in our lives.

Let's define it like this: "When we start reasoning in our own mind and leaning only toward our own understanding, then we are worshiping our own ability to work it out."

Our mind and our intellect have become our gods and we are in idolatry, because we have left Him out, for He said *"You shall have no other gods before me".* Exodus 20:3 NKJV

What is the solution? Repent and have your thinking line up with God's thinking and then watch what wonderful things He will do with what He has already gifted you with.

Continue to develop every aspect of your life, but do it under the leading of the Holy Spirit and with the agenda that you are going *"to seek first the kingdom of God and His righteousness and all things will be added to you"* Matthew 6:33 KJV As you are seeking God's kingdom, remember that *"the kingdom of God is not meat and drink; but righteousness, and peace, and joy in the Holy Ghost"* Romans 14:17 KJV

There is also a wonderful promise in this scripture *"Do not be wise in your own eyes; fear the Lord and depart from evil, It will be **health to your flesh (navel) and strength to your bones"** Proverbs 3:7-8 NKJV.*

Could it be that some of our stomach problems come from trying to run our own life and worrying about every aspect of it, instead of going to our Lord who promised that *"He would never leave us nor forsake us"* Hebrews 13:5 NKJV?

Beloved, His heart for you is so sweet and He longs for you to be a vessel of honor and reveal His glory in the earth. (2 Timothy

81

2:21, Ephesians 1:17-24)

Praise & Worship

God has also given us praise as an antidote for depression, as stated in Isaiah *"the garment of praise for the spirit of heaviness"* Isaiah 61:3 NKJV. If you have gone to another substance to relieve depression and heaviness before you have gone to God, you are contrary to the will (thinking) of God and you need to repent!

We have ministered to many people that seem to just refuse to praise God, and yet they can not understand why they are still in bondage. Again, it is simple. To not praise our creator, redeemer, healer, deliverer and restorer is just plain rebellion! I often tell people, "if you are uncomfortable praising God in your church setting, then go drive around in your car with the windows rolled up and put on some worship and praise music and learn to gloriously praise God. Your freedom will follow!"

How can I be so sure? Because His word says so!

God gives us a specific warning in II Samuel 6:14-23 concerning passing judgment or being critical of people that are rowdy in their praise to God. Michal, Saul's daughter and the wife of King David mocked him and scorned him because he danced with such abandonment before the Lord. King David was overcome with joy that he was finally getting the Ark of the Covenant moved and he was whirling and dancing and leaping before the Lord! David had also put off the royal robes and put on the robe of a servant of God as an act of worship to Jehovah.

Michal's words to David were not only defiling, but demeaning, critical and accusatory. This woman who had loved David now despised him in her heart because she did not approve of the rowdy worship of his God. Her mocking words of sarcasm *"How glorious was the King of Israel today, uncovering himself today in the eyes*

82

of the maids of his servants, as one of the base fellows, shamelessly uncovers himself' (vs. 20) cost her dearly!

Her attitude and actions cost her because the word says she was barren till her death. In fact, the scriptures never mention her again!

Her own judgment cursed her!

In this hour, God is clearly speaking a very sober word to be very careful about what you judge and what you criticize. It seems to be almost a trend in some Christian circles to widely criticize those Saints who are dancing, leaping and praising before the Lord. Usually this type of criticism comes because the people don't have understanding (only tradition) or revelation as to what God is doing. In ministry, I have seen the devastation that this judgment brings on people and it is mostly Christians that I have been dealing with. It is very real! I know this first hand, as I use to criticize, but now I am one of the leapers and dancers worshiping before my God who has redeemed, delivered, baptized, restored and healed me!

When the Lord touches you, as he touched the lame man in Acts 3 through the words of Peter and John, you won't have any trouble entering the church *walking, leaping and praising God* Acts 3:1-10 NKJV. No, it will be natural! Praise His wonderful name!

When we think like God thinks and we see praise and worship as He sees it then we will have no issues, but will only rejoice with those who are rejoicing. I have often heard people say: well, that is just not my way to be excited before God. My question to them is often this?

Are you born again and know Jesus as Lord?

Has God touched you?

Do you know Him in a deeper way that just intellectual?

Have you received the baptism of the Holy Spirit?

Have you witnessed His power?

Are signs and wonders a part of your life?
Are you leading the lost to the savior?
Are you living in victory?

If you answered "yes" to any or all of these then you should be excited about your walk with the Lord and rejoice in praise and worship to the King of Kings and the Lord of Lords!

Again, programming enters into this equation as many of us were raised in a church environment that said a church service should be a solemn assembly, and solemn they were. For us it then becomes very hard to be more vocal and demonstrative in worship, but God can set you free!

Taking God's Glory

How can we take God's glory? Simply by not giving God the credit that only belongs to him. This issue of taking God's glory has, throughout the history of the church, wrecked many fine men and women. Not only their ministries, but their lives as well have been destroyed. Father God made it clear that he would not give His glory to another (Isaiah 42:8, 48:11), but the pride of man is so strong that he is often trapped into the deception that he is the one responsible for the gifting, the anointing and the ministry that is flowing through him.

I like the way the Welshman minister, Arthur Burt, put it "By glory we mean credit due. God cannot share the glory because all things are *of Him and Him alone.* He would virtually deny Himself. This He cannot do (II Timothy 2:13). If only half the work is God's, then half the credit is God's; but if all the work is God's, then all the glory is God's".

"The scriptures do not put God's possession of the glory in the future tense. Thine is the glory, not Thine will be the glory! The glory never leaves His hand. While man seeks to rob God of His glory, there is a divine thermostatic control that operates as soon as man attempts to touch it".

"Just as the thermostat automatically controls the flow of cool air in a home, so God, the God of circumstances – of whom are all things – has everything under His control. His glory never leaves His hand".

Taken from Arthur Burt's book *"Surrender, Your Key to Spiritual Success"* published by Charisma House, copyright 1997, page 40, paragraphs 2, 3 & 4. Used by permission.

Paul has a strong admonition reminding us that all the things that happened in the Old Testament were for examples to us, that we might walk in wisdom and truth. He said *"Now all these things happened to them as examples, and they were written for our admonition (instruction & warning), upon whom the ends of the ages have come".* (I Corinthians 10:11 NKJV)

Let's look at the life of Uzziah, which is a prime example of how pride and taking God's glory will destroy our ministry and life.

The story of King Uzziah is found in II Chronicles 26. In verses 4&5 it says of Uzziah, *"that he did what was right in the sight of the Lord, according to all that his father Amaziah had done. He sought God in the days of Zechariah, who had understanding in the visions of God;* **and as long as he sought the Lord, God made him to prosper"** NKJV.

In verse 8 it says that *"he became exceedingly strong,* but in verse 15 the tone changes and it says *"that he was marvelously helped **till he became strong"*** NKJV.

In all his great and mighty accomplishments, King Uzziah forgot that God was the one behind his success, and he became proud of the accomplishments as if they were his alone. In other words, he started taking the glory unto himself that was God's alone!

What did this pride cost him? His kingdom and his life!

The story follows in verses 16 through 21 saying that *"When Uzziah was strong his heart was lifted up, to his destruction, for he transgressed against the Lord his God by entering the temple of the Lord to burn incense on the altar of incense"* NKJV.

Then when the priests tried to correct him and save him we see that Uzziah made a bad situation worse. The pride in him released his anger to flow against the priests for having the audacity to correct him. Remember a prideful man cannot receive correction and in Uzziah's case it was the last straw. He was then judged!

*"Then Uzziah became furious; and he had a censor in his hand to burn incense. And while he was angry with the priests, leprosy broke out on his forehead, before the priests in the house of the Lord, beside the incense altar. And Azariah the chief priests and all the priests looked at him, and there on his forehead, he was leprous; so they thrust him out of that place. Indeed he also hurried to get out, **because the Lord had struck him**"* NKJV.

Who struck him? The Lord struck him because he was trying to take God's glory as his own. Also he did not respond to correction, but lost his temper! Beloved, this is serious business!

"King Uzziah was a leper until the day of his death. He dwelt in an isolated house, because he was a leper; for he was cut off from the house of the Lord" NKJV

We may not like it, but the only solution to the issue of pride in our lives is to humble ourselves! We know that the pride of satan was what got him judged. He made the classic mistake of believing that he, the created one, could do a better job than, He the creator! We also will make that same mistake if we do not flow in love and accountability with other humble Christians who are concerned about our well being, and willing to correct us!

Remember my unscientific study on pride in the chapter on tranquilizers?

Well, one of the main things that all of these men had in common, whether they were ministers, professionals or craftsman, was that not one of them was in a true accountability relationship! In other words, they did not trust anyone (fear of man) enough to allow them to be blunt and honest with them. Consequently, they suffered because of the pride working in them that said they could handle it alone! But it will never work!

Other issues contrary to God!

Here are some other issues that are contrary to God's nature recorded in II Timothy 3:2-5 from the New King James Version for our consideration.

> lovers of themselves
> lovers of money
> boasters
> proud
> blasphemers
> disobedient to parents
> unthankful
> unholy
> unloving
> unforgiving or irreconcilable
> slanderers
> without self-control
> brutal
> despisers of good
> traitors
> headstrong
> haughty
> lovers of pleasure rather than lovers of God
> holding to a form of godliness, but denying its power

All of these issues need to faced head on and dealt with in order that we can enter into the joy of the Lord!

CHAPTER SIX

THE THREE TYPES OF SIN

The realities of sin that I am sharing with you are very liberating. I have found that many people get so stressed out when they think that they may have a sin issue in their life that they can't hear anything else. Of course, we all are still fighting the good fight of faith and we all want to be vessels of honor. But to be a vessel of honor we must deal with those things that are contrary to the nature of God.

The three types of sin are:

1- We were born into and live in a sin-cursed world.

I learned this many years ago as a policeman.

Kelley and I were working patrol in the northern district of town and had to go to the hospital to take a wreck report from an accident that had just cleared. Kelley was talking to one of the wreck victims, when Jane the lead nurse for the ER said to me "Ish, will you please talk to this woman and see if you can help her"? She led me down the hall and into an examining room where there was a lady bleeding from a head wound and also a little blond haired boy of about 5 years old sort of hiding behind the examining table.

Jane said "I know that these folks are not even in your district, but I don't know what to do with them". She continued "The father, a high ranking city official, struck her with an iron". I said, "But Jane, I can't take that report; it needs to be an officer from that district, and probably a domestic violence officer."

"Ish, she said, "I don't care about the report. I just want you to talk to her and calm her down, and see if there is somewhere she can go besides home". Nurse Jane knew how the system worked, and therefore knew that the abusive husband could be bailed out of jail and back at home before this traumatized woman left the ER.

I went in and talked to the lady and made arrangements for someone to take care of her till the situation was defused. That was when I got the revelation.

While I was talking to the mother, my partner Kelley was talking to the little boy, who I could now see was also bloody. Before he had been turned from me and partially hidden behind the examining table.

Kelly was letting the little guy play with his night stick and his handcuffs, when suddenly I noticed that tears were running down Kelley's face. I knew Kelley well and also knew that he was hard as nails and he was the best guy to have around when things got dicey. So what gives here? Kelley crying! It just was not computing until the little boy turned completely around and was now facing me. Then I knew what Kelley was upset about.

This little blond haired innocent kid, who had been assaulted by his father with an iron, was blind. The assault did not blind him. No, he was born blind, and yet this father had assaulted him and the mother with an iron.

I really cried out to the Lord that night and asked Him "Lord,

90

Why would this sort of thing happen"? He answered me in that still small voice and said "It is because we live in a sin-cursed world."

I had to ponder that for a while, but it set me free to understand those things that are not understandable. Suddenly I understood why little children die and are diseased. I understood why there are devastating natural circumstances like hurricanes, tornadoes, earthquakes and the like. These things happen because we live in a sin cursed world, and we have an enemy that, although defeated, is battling against creation to bring us as much misery and destruction as he can.

The more I prayed the more I saw that man is given "free choice" by God, and that means "free choice"!

In other words, even before Adam and Eve were in the garden, God made the decision that He was going to allow them to make their own choices. God, in His sovereignty, chose to give mankind his own sovereignty, or the ability to make our own choices. And God will not violate His nature.

Some had said that God does not always get His way, using the fact that God said *"He desires all men to be saved and to come to the knowledge of the truth"* I Timothy 2:4 NAS. Is God somehow fooled when people decide to reject Him and His love for them so clearly demonstrated on Calvary? No! God is never fooled, and He always gets His way! God got His way before the foundation of the world when He made the decision to give us the right to choose between life and death. God got His way, now it's up to us which way we will choose.

We are not robots!

Robots we are not, and who would want to be? Is God grieved

91

when we choose to go the wrong way? Yes, of course He is! But His decision long ago assured us that we would be the one making the choice. In His love, the choices are clearly put before us. That was God's will for each of us and He is indeed sovereign!

The Lord Jesus clearly gave us the authority and power to make the choice to serve Him or reject Him when He stated: *"But to as many as did receive and welcome Him, He gave the authority (power, privilege, right) to become the children of God, that is to believe in— adhere to, trust in and rely on—His name"* John 1:12 AMP.

God did not want robots! He would have made robots if that was His desire. But God created us to have fellowship with Him, and He knew that you can't have meaningful fellowship with a robot. To have a meaningful relationship you have to be able to choose to have the relationship, not forced into the relationship.

We are still allowed to make our own choices and that can cause tremendous suffering, particularly when someone else chooses to sin against us. And that brings us to sin area number two

2- We can be the victims of someone else's sin.

This is what had happened to this cute little boy. It was not his sin that hurt him, but his father's choice to sin that hurt the child. Was the child hurt? Yes! Both physically and emotionally was he damaged? If those wounds and offences are left unattended they will fester and erupt sooner or later. It is particularly damaging when it is a father that wounds you, because he has been ordained by God to protect you. If a child cannot feel safe with his own Father, then who can he feel safe with? The damage is tremendous, but I have seen hundreds of people set free from those wounds as they come into proper relationship with their Father God.

I am sure that all of us can identify with this and have our own stories. In fact, I have told the story of little Susie many times and there are always people in the audience that tell me that the story was their story as well.

In seminars I have demonstrated this concept of being victimized by finding someone on the front row that is a good sport. I will walk up to them and simulate kicking them in the shin. I then ask the audience, whose sin was that? Mine the kicker, or theirs, the kicked? There immediate reply is that it is my sin. The person sitting on the front row is innocent. Yet their have been bruised by the kicker's sin. In other words they have been victimized by someone else's sin.

I was demonstrating this in a church in the west and using a young lady sitting on the front row as my victim. Every time I did it the tears would start rolling down her face. At the break she told me that the reason that it was so emotional for her was that as a child her father would kick her in the shin as a form of punishment.

Many of us live in what I call "a little pink house with a white picket fence around it". We live in such a sheltered place, that we have no clue of the horror and devastation that face many children in our own country the USA. Having served as a policeman, police chaplain and in ministry I have seen first hand the damage done to people, and frankly, it is sickening.

A few recent statistics will verify what I am talking about.

In my home State, North Carolina, alone there were 31,000 cases of abused children in 2003. Those numbers only include the ones that we know about. Reality is that there are many more abuses that are never reported. And how would you ever calculate the verbal and emotional abuse that is done to youngsters?

5 children a day die!

According to a recent report there are 5 children killed each day in America! That is over 1,800 kids per year that die in their own homes! Unthinkable and unacceptable are these figures. That actually means that more kids die each day in their own home than the number of US soldiers that are killed each day in the current war in Iraq.

Here are some other statistics that may shock you. Every day in America these tragic things take place.

6 teens commit suicide
500 adolescents begin using drugs
3,610 teens are assaulted
80 are raped
1,000 unwed teenage girls become mothers
4,219 teenagers contact sexually transmitted diseases

Like it or not, we live in a violent society where life is no longer precious and respected.

Church, these are important issues because the church has the answer. The world is looking for it, in fact Romans says: *"For (even the whole) creation (all nature) waits expectantly and longs earnestly for God's sons to be known—waits for the revealing, the disclosing of their sonship"* Romans 8:19 AMP.

We have the answer and His name is Jesus. And we have the same Holy Spirit that raised Jesus from the dead living in us to help bring about restoration, healing and deliverance.

What are we waiting for? Let's press in to the King of Kings and Lord of Lords and deal with "stuff" so that the world can see His glory in the earth as they see His glory in us!

Now here is where the third aspect of sin can come in, and that is how you respond to offences.

3- Your own personal sin

Again, it is all about choice!

94

The gal sitting on the front row that was the victim of my play acting has to make a choice if that was real life. What are her choices? Well, she can choose to forgive her kicker, or she can choose to hate the kicker and hold resentment and bitterness toward him.

In this gal's case she said that she had hated her dad for this abuse, and though she had longed to have a proper relationship with him, the damage was too distant and too great. I hear stories like this frequently and I always have the same answer. Forgive your kicker!

In her case her dad had been dead for a number of years, but we still led her to forgive him and release him from those sins, and she was restored to her Father God. This was very important, because in her testimony she shared that she was not just mad at her dad, but also mad at God!

By the way, forgiving your kicker does not mean that you allow the kicker to keep kicking you. No, you make proper Godly boundaries between you and the offender in order to protect yourself. God never meant for you to be someone's punching bag!

Usually when personal sin is mentioned, people think about things like murder, stealing, adultery and the like. I am sure that we would agree that those issues are sins. But those sins are easily recognizable because they are so flagrant. The personal sins I am referring to are like *"the little foxes that spoil the vines"* Song of Solomon 2:15 NKJV, those *little foxes* that you don't even see in your own life. Those things that are hidden from you, which you are blind to, that you have justified or denied away. These are the subtle killers of your spiritual life and, quite possibly, your body as well.

Remember the pastor that had anger and bitterness toward a family member?

And do you recall the woman that didn't know that it was an issue to be mad at her sisters for twenty years?

Oh, and don't forget little Susie who didn't see anything wrong with hating herself and cursing herself.

What did each of these people have in common with each other?

1- They all loved God and were serving Him out of a pure heart.

2- They all had sin issues (little foxes) that were spoiling there lives.

3- None of these three dear people recognized the issue as a problem or as a sin.

The "little foxes" are things that we often pass off as bad emotions, but in reality they are issues that are contrary to God, and therefore they are sins against His nature.

Things such as bitterness, self bitterness, shame, guilt, rejection, performing in order to be approved by man , ungodly grief, keeping family secrets, unfulfilled expectations and broken dreams, disappointments, envy, jealousy, false burden bearing, worry, anxiety, fear, fabricated personality. All of these issues will put you in the "red zone" destroying your peace and destroying your mind and body.

Often we are blaming God or accusing God for our own choices that have been ungodly.

He has said it over and over that listening to Him and obeying His voice was life and life abundantly. He has exhorted us to make the right choices and those choices always bring life!

What happens when we decide by our own God given free will to make wrong, evil or dumb choices?

Look at this story that illustrates this concept and principle.

Dateline: Charlotte, N.C.

The picture on the front page of the paper was sad indeed! An obviously distraught and disheveled woman was standing broken and weeping in front of a burned down house.

Under this picture the caption read: "Why me Lord?

She was quoted as saying "I loved my children! Why did God do this to me? I have tried to live a good life, I go to church. Why did God let this happen to me?"

The writer told the story:

This woman had returned home in the early morning hours after partying and bar hopping with friends. She came home drunk to find that the house she shared with her boyfriend and three children had burned down. Two of her three children had perished in the fire. Her live-in boyfriend had also died. The third child was saved by a neighbor. They determined that the fire was started by a burning cigarette in the easy chair that the boy friend was sitting in. The blaze was consistent with the pattern that he was overcome by the smoke after having passed out. The fire department confirmed that a dropped cigarette by the drunken boyfriend was the cause of the fire.

The woman had asked, "Why did God do this to me and Why did God let this happen?"

Did God do that to her? Kill her children, burn her house down, force her and her boyfriend to drink them selves into oblivion? No, of course not! The answer is emphatically No! But God was being blamed, accused and railed against!

Well, if God didn't do it was someone responsible? Yes!

She did it by the choices she willingly made! This woman was not created a robot, but a real person with a free will and the ability to make moment by moment life choices.

She had been listening to the voice of the destroyer and he had succeeded over the years in slowly destroying her life and also her children. Yes, she lived in a sin cursed world and I am sure that she was many times a victim, but ultimately she made devastating wrong choices.

Some of you may think that I am being hard and callous, but beloved this is reality and we need to face it.

Never forget that it is only by His mercy and grace that we are not all in the same boat as this woman. I know that I thank God every day for sparing my life in those times when I was led by a "spirit of stupid" and made bad and potentially deadly decisions!

"Therefore let him who thinks he stands take heed lest he fall". II Corinthians 10:12 NKJV

Principle of Sowing and Reaping

"Do not be deceived, God is not mocked; for whatever a man sows, that he will also reap" Galatians 6:7 NKJV.

Often this scripture is used in teaching about giving and tithing, and that is certainly true. But the principle is also true with every aspect of our life. We are constantly sowing and we are constantly reaping, but it is not always negative.

Hosea said in sowing for positive:
> *"Sow for yourselves righteousness,*
> *Reap in mercy:*
> *Break up the fallow ground,*
> *For it is time to seek the Lord,*
> *Till He comes and rains righteousness on you"*
> Hosea 10:12 NKJV.

This principle of choosing (sowing) continues in Proverbs that reveals the negative:

"Then they will call upon me, But I will not answer: They will seek me diligently, But they will not find me. Because they hated knowledge And did not **choose** *the fear of the lord, They would have none of my Counsel and despised my every rebuke.* **Therefore they shall eat the fruit of their own way, And be filled to the brim with their own fancies"** Proverbs 1:28-31 NKJV.

Again the Psalmist says it:

But my people **would not heed** *My voice, And Israel would have none of Me. So I gave them over to their own stubborn heart,* **To walk in their own counsels.** *Oh, that My people would listen to Me, that Israel would walk in* **My ways, I would soon subdue their enemies and turn my hand against their adversaries"** Psalms 81:11-14 NKJV.

Reality was that this poor woman was not making *right choices,* and *therefore she ate the fruit of her own way and was filled to the brim with her own fancies.*

She **chose** to **listen** to and **obey** the destructive voice of the enemy rather than *heed* **God's** *voice.* She was *then given over to her own stubborn heart to walk in her own counsel* and that destroyed her.

The promise is clear that *if we would listen to the Lord and walk in His ways, then He would subdue our enemies and turn His hand against our adversaries.*

This woman reminds me of the woman at the well. No doubt, she had many challenges in her life, and my heart goes out to her and the millions like her that desperately need a tender touch from our Lord Jesus. **There is never room for condemnation;**

99

there is only room for love, mercy and grace.

I love the translation of II Timothy 2:24-26 that is in "The Message"

It says: *"God's servant must not be argumentative, but a gentle listener and a teacher who keeps cool, working firmly but patiently with those who refuse to obey (oppose themselves). You never know how or when God might sober them up with a change of heart and a turning to the truth, enabling them to escape the Devil's trap, where they are caught and held captive, forced to run his errands."*

Church, this book is being written help those who have *opposed themselves* and then help train those of us who are called to deliver, heal and restore the broken hearted!

This is the hour of **"Restoring Hearts, not condemning them"**!

CHAPTER SEVEN

THE BIG "IF"

"**IF**"——— is a big key to understanding the simplicity of what we are talking about! **IF** you can get a hold of this, your life will be changed.

This is not a formula! This is not science! This is not a system! It is truth!

IF is simply bringing the spiritual together with the natural and medical to understand how disease and torment have gained access to our minds and bodies.

Spiritual roots

Some people have referred to this as spiritual roots, and I would certainly agree with that term. But we have to be careful, because every sickness is not caused by what I would call spiritual roots.

There are some teachings on spiritual roots that say that all sickness and disease come from a spiritual root in your own life. I would have to disagree with that premise. It leaves out the fact that we live in a sin-cursed world, and sometimes bad stuff just happens because we live in a sin cursed world.

There are many aspects to this sin-cursed world. One being that through the sin of greed (man's choice) man has destroyed the soil, and now what we get in our grown food is even questionable as to nutritional value. And I shudder to think what poison I am ingesting as I drink water every day, and even some bottled water is no better.

There are also those issues that are passed down through the family lines. It is for that reason when you go to the Doctor he asks you all kinds of questions about your family tree. Well, the same thing is true in your spiritual family tree. That which is true in the natural can be also true in the spiritual.

Another major issue that I have encountered is that when people start focusing on spiritual roots that they can become trapped. It is sort of like "seeking the gifts and not the giver".

Also very damaging is the condemnation that the devil and his little helpers (Christians with a little knowledge, but very little grace and wisdom) can put on people with faulty understanding of spiritual roots. I have known people that became so focused on the root issues that it became a science to them. These dear sick folks were on a constant search for that "elusive root" that seemed to always be just out of reach. Consequently they had lost their joy.

Sin conscious verses God conscious!

This search for the elusive root can become a form of works or performance, neither of which is fruitful. Improper focusing on roots can also lead to being "sin or evil conscious". And that is not fruitful. We need to become God conscious. It is a trick of the enemy to provoke us to become conscious of anything that takes us away from the Father, Son and Holy Spirit's love for us. This type of improper emphasis can put you in the "red zone" and cause you to lose your peace. This was true of both the ministry teachers and the ones receiving the ministry.

Beloved, this is not a science. It is about our relationships with God, our relationship with our self and our relationship with other people. There are times we just don't have a clue what is going on, and then we should press into the Savior, the Redeemer, the Healer and the Lord who desires to set you free. Jesus can do it! Cry out to Him!

We also have to look at the examples of healing that Jesus performed as He walked the earth. We know that many of the people had spiritual roots that may have caused the issue, but Jesus just goes after the disease or evil spirit and deals with it. That should be our pattern as well.

A few examples would be:

Peter's mother in-law healed. Matthew 8:14
Demon possessed delivered and healed. Matthew 8:16
As many as touched Him were made well. Mark 7:56
Blind Bartimaeus was healed. Mark 10:46-52
Multitude healed and delivered. Luke 6:17-19
Woman healed of spirit of infirmity. Luke 13:10-17
Woman at the well healed. John 4:7-25
Man healed at the pool of Bethesda John 5:1-9

Sometimes we have to lovingly spend the time with folks and teach them, build faith in them and counsel with them so that they can receive their healing and deliverance.

A good example of this would be Matthew 17 where Jesus had to instruct or counsel regarding the sin of unbelief and how that sin had affected the generations.

In this one story Jesus taught about the following issues:

1-deliverance

2-healing

3-spiritual roots of unbelief

4-the interplay of sickness and demonic power

5-theology of healing and health

6-generational curses in the family line

7-prayer

8-fasting

9-faith!

Many times we have to do the same and that is why we encourage people to attend a seminar or conference for the impartation of truth and life prior to prayers for healing.

So here comes the **"IF"**

"IF" there is a spiritual root involved in your sickness or torment, then wouldn't you like to identify the **"IF"** and deal with it? Of course you would!

Ok, first let's define what we mean by spiritual roots. Webster Dictionary defines root as *"that from which something derives its origin, growth or life."*

It also defines root as *"providing support or underground growth"*

What is underground growth? It is a "root"!

Spiritual could be defined as that which is spiritual as opposed to that which is just natural.

So taking these two words together we can see that something spiritual is providing support, provoking an underground origin, growth or life! Ok, let's take it a step further and say that the dynamic that is causing the root is something contrary to God's thinking and therefore a sin if we are involved!

Let's say it this way, and give this as a definition *"that a spiritual dynamic (sin issue) is providing support or a root and giving the disease or torment growth or life"*

Definition of "SIN"

Sin can be defined in many accurate ways such as:
  *Missing the mark
  *Rebellion against God
  *Disobedience of His word
  *Transgression of God's authority
  *All Unrighteousness

There are many ways to define sin, but to make my point I want to tell you a true story that I trust will illustrate sin to you. It certainly brought it home for me.

My plumbing story

Some years ago I was serving as a teaching pastor at Pleasant Valley Church a church that dealt specifically with spiritual roots and relational issues. The ministry was awesome and we were seeing lives changed regularly through the teaching and ministry of one week schools. Our schedule was very intense and our days off were few, and sometimes far between.

One Sunday afternoon, as a family, we were all sitting around enjoying each other's company. My wife Tonda was washing some clothes. I was very relaxed sitting on the couch with my two pre teen age daughters Taylor and Lexie. Suddenly, we all heard water back up into the kitchen sink and Tonda immediately turned off the washing machine.

I went to the kitchen sink and sure enough there was soapy water that had backed up into the sink. Not a good sign!

I made a quick decision and told Tonda "Don't worry! let's just keeping washing the clothes"! Some people would call that denial, but we were having such a good time that I did not want to be interrupted to do something which I knew nothing about, and that is plumbing. So she started again and the sink filled up again! This time it almost ran over the top of the deep sink onto the floor, so I knew that I was in trouble. Then we checked the other sinks and the toilets and they were also backing up! No more denying that we had a problem!

The reality was I now had four problems!

1- I am not a plumber!

2- We had a plumbing problem!

3- I am slowly losing my peace that I was enjoying sitting on the couch!

4- I am the head of the house and a love covering for my wife and children so I am responsible to get it fixed!

Well, since I am not a plumber, I called my neighbor, Richard Garrett who is one of those wonderful people that can fix any thing! Well, now I had another problem. Richard was not home!

Ok, now I called the maintenance man from the church that lived near by. Well, now I had problem number five, because he was not at home either! Remember, we had been working long hours and this was the first time in quite a while that we had sat down as a family, and now that time was getting messed up by a plumbing problem. My attitude was changing, but not for the better.

Ok, I am now moving quickly into the "If-Then syndrome" and my peace is dissipating!

I was fine and moving in the peace of the Lord as long as everything was ok, but now I have a plumbing problem and I am not a plumber! For me, it does not get much worse!

It is decision time! I can either move out of the house into a motel, or I can try to fix it myself. Frankly, the motel idea was very appealing, but just was not practical, so under the house I go to make an appearance of trying to fix it.

Remember, I am not a plumber, but I did know that there was a clean out valve under the house. I figured that I could open that and drain the back up stuff and maybe that would do it. Then we could get back to enjoying the day.

It was not to be!

I found the clean out valve and sat before it with my big pliers to wrestle it open. And wrestle it I did. Now, I had never done this before and I did not realize that if I am sitting right in front of the drain out valve that it would be a problem. It quickly became problem number six! I was drenched with the plumbing water!

What had started out as a quiet well-deserved, relaxing afternoon with my family was quickly getting worse and worse! I had started entering the "red zone" when the water backed up in the sink, but now I was up to about number seven on the chart!

Now, my peace level was going down quickly and my "red zone" was going up, but I did not give up. I gathered Tonda, Taylor and Lexie and gave them this plan.

I would go back under the house with a stiff garden hose and I would run the garden hose up the drain until it reached the blockage. When I gave them the signal they would turn on the water and hopefully the water would clear the blockage. Tonda was controlling the water and Taylor and Lexie were stationed at the hatch doors to hold them open for light.

"Don't sit in front of the drain lesson"
It was a good plan except I might as well have spoken to Tonda

in tongues without the interpretation because I wanted her to just turn on the water a little bit. But I didn't say that so she turned on the water full blast! Well, full blast would have been ok, except that I had not learned the "don't sit in front of the drain lesson", and no sooner did that water surge through that hose and hit the blockage than it made an immediate return and landed on me with a vengeance! Even my shoes were now full! Yuck!

I have now got problem number eight! I am no longer experiencing any peace. It is all gone and I am in full blown number ten "red zone"! At this level you are dangerous to everyone including yourself!

Well, I lost it. Lost what? My temper! I started yelling for Tonda to turn off the water. From where she was she could not hear me, so I started yelling at the kids to tell her to turn off the water. The situation was now totally out of control and I was yelling so loud that I almost lost my voice! Not good!

When I started yelling my kids scattered like a covey of quail and Tonda waited patiently for me to come out from under the house.

I am sure that I looked funny covered from head to toe and shoes full and running over with drain water, but I did not see the humor in it. At the same time, I knew that I had defiled my wife and kids and needed to get it straightened out. That was problem number nine.

It gets worse!

I wanted to apologize and get it right by asking them to forgive me for losing it and yelling at them, but instead I said to Tonda, "Well, you did the best you good".

Was that an apology? No! It was stubborn pride talking! And so now you have defilement on top of defilement!

Here I am a pastor teaching these principles of "repentance and forgiveness" on a weekly basis and I can't even do it, because of my pride!

Unrighteous Judgment of others!

You may ask, Why was I mad at them? It was not their fault! Well, in my unrighteous judgment it was their fault. I had made the assumption that the drain was backed up because with three gals in the house I knew that all kinds of things can go down the drain that are not suppose to. You know things like hair, fingernails, barrettes and hair nets. Who knows what might be down there.

So I had started blaming them before I ever went under the house for my baptism, and the longer the story played out the madder I got because of my unrighteous judgment.

I know that it does not sound very spiritual, but beloved it is reality!

Now I choose to add problem number ten by going to bed while still being angry. Really not good!

Paul said to the Ephesians: *"Be angry, and do not sin: do not let the sun go down on your wrath, nor give place to the devil. Let him who stole steal no longer, but rather let him labor, working with his hands what is good, that he may have something to give him in need. Let no corrupt word proceed out of your mouth, but what is good for necessary edification, that it may impart grace to the hearers. And do not grieve the Holy Spirit of God, by whom you were sealed for the day of redemption. Let all bitterness, wrath, anger, clamor (loud quarreling), and evil speaking be put away from you, with all malice. And be kind to one another, tenderhearted, forgiving one another, even as God in Christ Jesus forgave you"* Ephesians 4:26-32 NKJV.

Obviously I did not sleep very well and got up with a throbbing headache. Unrepentant sin will do that! I headed for the church and at 7:00am I was sitting in my office trying to get going and not being very successful. Another pastor, a dear friend of mine, stuck his head in the door and invited me to listen to a praise song in his office. Honestly, that was the last thing I wanted to do at that moment, but remember you have to "wear the mask" so into his office I went.

My restoration!

That praise song was my deliverance and restoration! I don't even know what the song was, but when the song started I broke and started to weep! Oh glorious tears of repentance! The other pastor didn't think anything of my tears as he was weeping also. We often did that together, so it was not unusual.

I told the brother that I had to go home and take care of something, but before I could leave someone else walked in, and suddenly we were in a meeting. It was that way all morning. I was sitting there miserable. I wanted to go home to repent for my words and actions, and for restoration to take place. I couldn't leave because the meeting kept getting bigger.

Late that morning my wife came into the meeting, as she was part of the teaching staff. Now was the test and I had to choose to deal with it (*the sin and pride*) there in front of all these other staff members, or let it slide till later.

I made the right choice to deal with it there and asked to stop the meeting. In front of all those folks I asked Tonda to forgive me for my anger, my outburst of defiling words and for wounding her heart and the children's hearts! She looked at me with love and in front of all those people she said "Ish, I have already forgiven you"!

I then said "Will you release me from the sin that I have committed against you and the girls"? She said "Yes I release you in the

110

name of Jesus, from the defilement, the words and the sins against us". Later that afternoon I was able to also ask the girls to forgive me, and they did.

The release was almost overwhelming as I experienced the grace of God at that moment!

I knew that now I was back in fellowship with my family and with my God. Now the headache was gone and I was refreshed!

At that time I remembered the words of Jesus when He said *"Whoever seeks to save his life will lose it, and whoever loses his life will preserve it"* Luke 17:33 NKJV. Those are powerful words that revealed to me if I would humble myself in front of those people and *"lose my life"* that He would restore my life, and He did!

To conclude this story we find out that the blockage was caused by the septic tank being totally filled up. When that happens there is a flapper valve that closes and it cannot be opened. The only way to get it opened is too clean out the septic tank. So, we called that service that we nicknamed the "honey wagon" and they came and cleaned out the septic tank. Then we were back in business.

Were my actions and words sins? Yes! No doubt about that. But let's look at it from a kingdom perspective.

Two Kingdoms

We know that Satan wants to manifest his nature and evil destructive intentions throughout the earth, and he uses people to do his work, whether we are aware of it or not! Here are some of the other names that satan is known as in the scriptures:

*Abaddon, Rev 9:11

*Accuser of the brethren, Rev. 12:10

*Angel of the bottomless pit, Rev 9:11

*Adversary, I Peter 5:8

*Apollyon, Rev.9:11

111

*Beelzebub, Matt.12:24, Mark 3:22, Luke 11:15

*Belial, 2 Cor. 6:15

*Devil, Matt 4:1, Luke 4:2,6; Rev 3:20

*Father of lies, John 8:55

*The enemy, Matt 13:39

*Great red dragon, Rev 12:3

*Liar, John 8:44

*Lucifer, Is.14:12

*King of Tyrus, Ezek.28:12-15

*Murderer, John 8:44

*Old serpent Rev 12:9

*Prince of this world, John 12:31, 14:30, 16:11

*Prince of the devils, Matt. 12:24

*Prince of the power of the air, Eph. 2:2

*Satan, I Chr. 21:1, Job 1:6, John 13:27, Acts 5:3, 26:18, Romans 16:20

*Tempter, Matt. 4:3, I Thess. 3:5

*The god of this world, II Cor. 4:4

*Wicked one Matt.13:19, 39

*Evil one Matt 6:13

In bible times people were named based on their nature. The devil's horrendous nature is revealed by his names. And we can usually recognize the devil's work by many of theses names. For instance if you are accusing or being accused (the accuser, Rev 12:10) it is of his evil nature (luciferian) and is a manifestation of the devil's work. If you participate, then you have agreed with the devil and now you have become a partaker of the sin! Yikes! Not very pretty! How about lying? The same spiritual principle would apply. If you lie (liar John 8:44) then you are in agreement with the work of the enemy, and it has become your sin, because you have become a conduit for the enemy's tactics. What are his tactics? To steal, kill and destroy!

We don't need to concentrate on the enemy, but we had better be aware that we have an enemy, and he wants to destroy us and deceive us. It is tragic to find the countless people that sit in pews Sunday after Sunday that will tell you that Satan is not real. All the while their lives are being destroyed.

"Big Mouth"

Has the devil been defeated? Yes! The devil was defeated at the cross! Then why do we have to be concerned with him? Because he is the original "big mouth" and he will try every trick to get you to listen to his garbage. If he can get you to listen he will wear you down until you give in and usually by that time you are not even aware of what is going on. His "big mouth" is running constantly, and your discernment (Hebrews 5:14) better be exercised and sharp or you will get trapped.

How can we be so sure? Because we have the examples in scripture that prove the point that "big mouth" is trying to get us into trouble. Let's look at four of them.

Adam & Eve

Is the serpent capable of forcing Adam and Eve to make a wrong choice? No! But he ran that "big mouth" long enough that they started doubting God's word and it cost them and us dearly. They were living in peace (homeostasis) until they chose to follow the enemy's words and then they lost their peace, stability, and fellowship with the Father all because of words! Genesis chapter 3

King David numbers Israel

Then we have the story of satan moving David to number

Israel in I Chronicles 21:1-30.

What happened? The enemy ran that "big mouth" and appealed to the pride in David that wanted to know how big he was, and how big his army was. As the Amplified version says it was David's *"reliance on human resources"* that displeased the Lord. It cost a pestilence against Israel and 70,000 men died! All because a "foothold" of pride turned into a "stronghold" of pride! David was listening to the wrong voice! His friend Joab tried in vain to reason with David, but pride will seldom reason, because pride is always right!

How many churches do we know of today that post their numbers all over the place? Their Sunday school numbers, prayer meeting numbers, church service numbers and membership numbers. Our focus needs to be on quality not quantity!

Judas

We are all familiar with the story of Judas betraying the Lord Jesus, but sometimes we forget that in John 13:2 it says these words. *"And supper being ended, the devil having already put it into the heart of Judas Iscariot, Simon's son to betray him"* How did the devil accomplish that? He simply kept putting the thought into Judas's mind until it took hold. What started as a "foothold became a stronghold"!

Ananias & Sapphira

The fourth example is the story of Ananias and Sapphira who sold property to help the church, but kept back part of it for themselves. The story goes like this: *"But a certain man named Ananias with his wife Sapphira sold a piece of property, And with his wife's knowl-*

edge and connivance he kept back and wrongfully appropriated some of the proceeds, bringing a part only and putting it at the feet of the apostles. But Peter said to Ananias, why has satan filled your heart that you should lie to and attempt to deceive the Holy Spirit, and should (in violation of your promise) withdraw secretly and appropriate to your own use part of the price from the sale of the land? As long as it remained unsold, was it not still your own? And (even) after it was sold, was not (the money) at your disposal and under your control? Why then is it that you have proposed and purposed in your heart to do this thing? How could you have the heart to do this deed? You have not (simply) lied to me—playing false and showing yourself utterly deceitful—but to God. Upon hearing these words, Ananias fell down and died. And great dread and terror took possession of all who heard of it. And the young men arose and wrapped up (the body) and carried it out and buried it. Now after an interval of about three hours his wife came in, not having learned of what had happened. And Peter said to her, Tell me; did you sell the land for so much? Yes, she said, for so much. Then Peter said to her, How could you two have agreed and conspired together to try to deceive the Spirit of the Lord? Listen! The feet of those who have buried your husband are at the door, and they will carry you out (also) and instantly she fell down at his feet and died, and the young men entering found her dead, and they carried her out and buried her beside her husband. And the whole church was appalled – great awe and strange terror and dread seized them – and all others who heard of these things" Acts 5:1-11 Amp.

What did Peter mean when he asked *"how has satan so filled your heart"*? How did satan fill their heart? By running that "big mouth" of the tempter! And they bought his story - hook, line and sinker, and it literally cost them their lives. Yes, the enemy is a liar, a tempter and a killer!

Can a Christian walk in darkness? Yes! Because God has given us a free will to choose death and life every day.

Can a Christian walk in darkness even after they have been born again? Yes, Absolutely! Well, what about after we have been filled with the Spirit Yes, absolutely! Did Paul not say *"Do not quench the Spirit"* I Thessalonians 5:19 NKJV and *"Do not grieve the Holy Spirit of God"* Ephesians 4:30 NKJV? Quenching and grieving would be walking in darkness!

Ask yourself the question as to whether or not you do any of the contrary things (sins) since you've been born again as you did before your were born again. Examples might be gossip, slander, backbiting, anger, quarrelling, strife, bad temper, pouting, etc.

Why do you still do them? I believe that we make wrong choices!

Well, what are our choices?

We have two! We can choose to serve the kingdom of God which is *life*, or we can choose to serve the luciferian kingdom, which is *death*! There is really no third choice!

We have to be on the alert and sober as to which kingdom we are serving at any given time in both our thoughts, words and actions!

Whose kingdom was I serving when I lost my temper at my wife and girls?

Whose kingdom was I serving when I let circumstances rule my life and peace?

Whose kingdom was I serving when I shouted at them and defiled them?

Whose kingdom was I serving when my own pride would not let me confess my sins? Whose kingdom was I serving when I went to bed angry?

I was not serving the kingdom of God at those times, but I was serving or manifesting another kingdom that is *luciferian* in nature.

And that became my SIN!!!

116

Call it what you want to, but it was **sin** and it was mine, and I was in trouble until I dealt with it! Part of that trouble or torment was that by my words and actions I was living in the "red zone", and was not sleeping and had a throbbing headache. *Repentance* brought back the peace that only comes when we are in right relationship with God, with ourselves and with each other.

So a definition of sin would be *"to allow the luciferian kingdom to manifest or reveal his nature through your life"*!

See the difference? It is "missing the mark", "rebellion against God", disobedience of His word", "transgression of God's word" and "all unrighteousness"; but it is more that that. It is *"to allow the luciferian kingdom to manifest or reveal his nature through your life"*.

That makes the picture ugly!

Do we want to manifest the kingdom of Satan? No! But that is exactly what we are doing when we allow sin to have its way in our life. God is not getting the glory, but the enemy is!

My sins toward my family were a violation of God's nature and word, and therefore I was out of fellowship with God and my family, and that caused me to lose my peace which put me in the "red zone". Truly, the only way out is *Repentance and Forgiveness!*

CHAPTER EIGHT

POWER OF THE TONGUE

The old saying "sticks and stones can break my bones, but words cannot hurt me" is just not true. Words can steal your joy, break your heart, and destroy close relationships! Words can kill you as surely as a gun can; it just takes a little longer.

"*Death and life are in the power of the tongue*" Proverbs 18:21 NKJV, and words of defilement will cause deep wounds. "*The words of a talebearer (gossip or slanderer) are like tasty trifles (wounds), and they go down into the inmost (rooms of the belly) body*" Proverbs 18:8, NKJV. "*A perverse man sows strife (competitive, quarreling, brawling contentious) and a whisperer (slanderer) separates the best of friends*" Proverbs 16:28 NKJV

In my ministry experience, I have seen far more damage done by gossip and slander than by things that some would consider more serious!

A definition of gossip would be: "*Telling someone something about someone else that doesn't affect you or concern you and you cannot do anything about it*". Those words then are gossip!

Words are often the means that the enemy uses to put curses on you in order to try and destroy you. These words, even though

119

they are lies, spoken to us can become proclamations that we believe and then act on.

For instance, a father, a mother, a teacher, a coach, a drill instructor, or a church authority can say to you "You will never amount to anything; you are a bum just like your daddy was".

Now if you accept these words as truth they will start becoming true because your body will respond to the words! Unfortunately, many people grow up hearing these demeaning proclamations on a daily basis, and they are literally being programmed to believe them.

Does this seem hard to believe? Remember little Susie? She believed that she was not special because of Johnny's actions and the subsequent words of the enemy that she was not significant or pretty.

Speech center in the brain!

It is a well known fact by the medical community that the speech center located in the brain actually controls the whole body! Yes, it literally has control over all the nerves of the body. Neurologists know that by speaking a word, either negative or positive, that those words can steer the body in either a negative or positive direction. The speech will actually cause the body to react. For instance, if you keep saying "I feel sick or I feel weak", well you will actually feel sick or weak, because your body picks up on what you say. Another example would be to *not* say that you are "retired", because when you do say you are "retired" your body picks up on it and will start shutting down. Why? Because "retired" means finished, over and done with. A pastor friend of mine said that a better thing to say is "I am re-treading"! I like that! Actually this is not new at all because the famous Dr. James said it two thousand years ago under the inspiration of the Holy Spirit.

"Who is this famous Dr. James?" Well Dr. James is the brother of Jesus and he clearly defines the activity and importance of the tongue and speech center. He defined it long before modern medical science understood it!

"The tongue is the least member of our body, but can bridle the whole body!

"For we all stumble in many ways. If any man does not stumble in what he says, he is a perfect man, able to bridle the whole body as well. Now if we put the bits into the horse's mouths so that they must obey us, we direct their entire body as well Behold the ships also, though they are so great and are driven by strong winds, are still directed by a very small rudder, wherever the inclination of the pilot desires. So also the tongue is a small part of the body, and yet it boasts of great things. Behold, how great a forest is set aflame by such a small fire! And the tongue is a fire, the very world of iniquity; the tongue is set among our members as that which defiles the entire body, and sets on fire the course of our life, and is set on fire by hell. For every species of beasts and birds, of reptiles and creatures of the sea, is tamed, and has been tamed by the human race. But no one can tame the tongue; it is a restless evil and full of deadly poison. With it we bless our Lord and Father; and with it we curse men, who have been made in the likeness of God; From the same mouth comes both blessing and cursing. My brethren, these things ought not to be this way. Does a fountain send out from the same opening both fresh and bitter water?Can a fig tree, my brethren, produce olives, or a vine produce figs? Neither can salt water produce fresh"
James 3:1-12,NAS.

Medicine, Science and the word of God line up!

These facts related here are undisputable and undeniable! Medicine, science and the word of God line up completely. They are totally in sync with each other. Has your tongue trapped you and even cursed you? If so, then now is the time to repent and start making your confession line up with the word of God!

This is exactly what happened to little Susie. At the age of 12 she started speaking negative words in her mind and out loud to the mirror, and her body responded to her commands just like Dr. James said it would!

Her words became a self-imposed curse on her life, and although it had taken many years for it to manifest into a disease, manifest it did.

Often I am asked, "But she was a Christian and *"old things have passed away, behold new things have come"* II Corinthians 5:17 NAS. How can that be? "

Yes! She was a Christian and was actually a Christian before the episode with Johnny. But that does not nullify the spiritual principle laid out by Dr. James and the others. The principle is still the same – *"Death and life are in the power of the tongue"*!

Sometimes our definitions are confused. Past does not necessarily mean in terms of time, but past needs to be in terms of "resolution". The definition of resolution, according to Webster, is *"An outcome or result that serves to settle a problem, uncertainty, or conflict."*

The situation with Susie was well over 25 years in her past, but was still very much a part of her present! In other words, it was not resolved or settled. Daily she was cursing herself, and even though those around her did not know it. She truly had no idea the damage she was doing to herself.

Why was it still in her past? The past was still there because she was holding bitterness toward herself for not being good enough, and anger towards God for not stopping the rejection and humiliation.

Often self pity will keep us in the past, and someone once

described self pity as the **"super glue of hell that binds you to the past!"**

Remember, we can have issues with God, others and ourselves.

Well, Susie had forgiven Johnny years ago, but she was still mad at God and herself!

She had a desperate need to forgive herself and release her wrong perception of God!

CHAPTER NINE

HOW DO WE FORGIVE?

Forgiveness can be a very difficult issue! We are all familiar with the offenses that have been thrown our way and how they pierce our heart and spirit, but often we don't comprehend the spiritual and emotional damage done to us through words and actions by others.

She was still struggling with anger at God and at herself! She still had unforgiveness toward herself and was holding the perception that somehow God had not been fair with her. So she was mad at God and herself!

It is easy just to tell people "Oh forgive so-n-so for offending you, slandering you, defiling you, abusing you, etc." But it is much harder to really do it!

And then it gets tricky, because many of us are holding on to past offenses and dwelling on them, and don't even realize it.

Remember the pastor that had the issue with an in-law? Well, he truly did not know that it was a spiritual issue (sin) of bitterness and unforgiveness, and he was in a place where you would have thought he knew better. But, that is proof positive just how clever and deep the deception can be in someone's life.

Was he in the "red zone" because of the unforgiveness that was in his life? Yes!

Was he sick because he was in unforgiveness and bitterness? Well, his testimony went like this. That the anger, frustration and bitterness had opened the door to disease, and that when he repented of the bitterness and anger toward the family member then healing in his body took place. He had to get his thinking lined up with God's thinking and then his body came into peace.

Did he need to forgive and repent? Yes! And it worked!

How about the woman that had not spoken to her sisters for over 20 years because they had gotten mad at each other after their mother's death? Did she have a bitterness and unforgiveness issue (sin) towards them? Yes!

Was she harboring this bitterness and unforgiveness toward them? Yes! Was she in the "red zone" because she was violating the spiritual principles of repentance and forgiveness? Yes!

Was she living in the "resistance stage of fight or flight" and consequently her body and mind was in turmoil? Yes! You bet it was and disease was at her door and had found a place to enter.

Did she need to forgive and repent? Yes!

Canceling a debt!

I look at forgiveness as canceling a debt that is owed to me!

Webster defines forgiveness as: 1- "to grant pardon for or remission of something." 2-"To cease to blame or feel resentment against someone or something for an offence"

The Greek word for forgive is *Aphiemi,* and it means: "to send away, 'to forgive debts, these debts to be completely canceled'; 'the deliverance of the sinner from the penalty'; 'bestow a favor unconditionally'; to loose or to release'; setting a person free"

126

In order for us to be free we must first release those who have sinned against us! We do it by canceling the debt that they owe us. We cancel it and never look for any kind of restitution from them.

Excuses to not forgive!

Many folks fail to find the peace through forgiveness because they have rationalized that they don't really have to forgive until certain things happen. Here are just a few of the excuses.

For instance, they say "**I won't forgive until I can forget**".

Well, you are going to be in the "red zone" a long time, because you may never forget the offence, but, praise God, you can be delivered from the pain of that memory. It may take some time, because you also have to deal with the grief of the offense and debt, but Jesus in you is your hope of glory and the pain will leave! I have seen that to be true 100's of times. It has worked for me and it will work for you as God is no respecter of persons!

Another one they use to not forgive is to say "**well, time will heal it**"

No it won't! In fact it will only continue to fester and get worse until you forgive. And all the while you are living in the "red zone", and your mind and body are breaking down.

The most damaging and deceptive one that I have seen is "**I'm waiting for them to come and admit they were wrong and tell me they are sorry, and then I will forgive them**"!

If you are waiting for that you may very well take that offence to the grave! And you may go earlier to the grave than is your appointed time, as you will be living in the "red zone" and your immune system will be wrecked!

I have had many people tell me "**that when God wants them to forgive the offender and the offence that He will give them the**

grace and faith to forgive".

Well, that may sound very spiritual, but the reality is that the Lord Jesus has given us a clear mandate to forgive, and He has already given us faith and grace. We already have all that we need to be partakers of the divine nature, which is the nature of the Son! You already have the Spirit of the living God in you and that is the same Spirit that raised Jesus from the dead. How much more do we need?

Sometimes it is really a matter of desire. **"Behind every excuse is a lack of desire" Do we really want to forgive?** Or are we enjoying holding onto the offences, and mulling the offences over and over, like a tape player?

Matthew 18

Is it easy? No! But it will release you from the torment that has plagued you since you took on the offense that caused you to be in anger, hostility, resentment and bitterness toward them.

Earlier we looked briefly at the story of Matthew 18, but let's look at it a little closer to see clearly the horrific results that we will reap if we refuse to forgive.

> Then Peter came and said unto him, "Lord, how often shall my brother sin against me and I forgive him? Up to seven times?"
> Jesus said to him, "I do not say to you, up to seven times, but up to seventy times seven.
> "For this reason the kingdom of heaven may be compared to a certain king who wished to settle accounts with his slaves.
> "And when he had begun to settle them, there was brought to him one that owed him 10,000 talents ($10,000,000).
> "But since he did not have the means to repay, his lord commanded him to be sold along with his wife and children and all that he had, and repayment to be made.
> "The slave therefore falling down, prostrated himself before him,

saying, 'Have patience with me, and I will repay you everything.'
"And the lord of that slave felt compassion and released him
and forgave him the debt.

"But that slave went out and found one of his fellow slaves who
owed him one hundred denarii's ($100.00); and he seized him and began
to choke him saying 'Pay back what you owe.'

"So his fellow slave fell down and begin to entreat him, saying,
'Have patience with me and I will repay you.'

"He was unwilling however, but went and threw him in prison
Until he should pay back what was owed.

"So when his fellow slaves saw what had happened, they were
deeply grieved and came and reported to their lord all that had hap-
pened.

"Then summoning him, his lord said to him, 'You wicked slave, I
forgave you all that debt because you entreated me.

"Should you not also have had mercy on your fellow slave, even
as I had mercy on you?"

"And his lord, moved with anger, handed him over to the tortur-
ers until he should repay all that was owed him.

"So shall My heavenly Father also do to you, if each of you does
not forgive his brother from your heart" Matthew 18:21-35 NAS.

Was this the only time that Jesus said something like this? No!
Remember that He taught in the Lord's Prayer to *"forgive us our*
debts, as we also have forgiven our debtors" Matthew 6:12 NAS.

Also, the powerful teaching by the Lord Jesus on moving
mountains by faith is followed by a sobering command and condition to answered prayer!

And Jesus replying said to them, "Have faith in God (constantly).
Truly, I tell you whoever says to this mountain, Be lifted up and thrown
into the sea! And does not doubt at all in his heart, but believes that what
he says will take place; it will be done for him. For this reason I am telling

*you, whatever you ask for in prayer, believe—trust and be confident—that it is granted to you, and you will (get it). And whenever you stand praying, if you have anything against any one, forgive him and **let it drop—leave it, let it go**—in order that your Father Who is in heaven may also forgive you your (own) failings and shortcomings and let them drop. But if you do not forgive, neither will your Father in heaven forgive your failings and shortcomings"* Mark 22:22-26 AMP.

Let it drop!

Beloved, here is the answer to forgiving! **You let it drop — leave it — let it go!**

We do it by the following the example of our Lord Jesus when he said of those who had so abused, mocked, tormented and tortured him *"Father, forgive them, for they do not know what they do"* Luke 23:34 NKJV.

Jesus in one sentence cancelled the debt that they owed him! Can we do the same to those who have offended us? Yes! But only through the power of the risen Lord that is working His love and grace in us!

You see, when we refuse to move and act as Jesus did then we are in rebellion against His word and His nature.

When we refuse to forgive, we are tying God's hands to move on our behalf and many prayers are going unanswered because we are not allowing His grace to flow through us.

Truth without action is only fraud!

We sometimes have this idea that God will just move on our behalf regardless of our actions. That is faulty thinking! No, we serve a holy God who has set before us spiritual principles for our own good, and when we refuse them we will reap the consequences of those choices. You see truth without action is only fraud!

In some ways this is all about whom and what we believe. If we believe God, then we will do what he asks of us, and if we don't believe God, then we won't do what He asked of us. Again, truth without action is only fraud!

A question we should ask ourselves at this point is: **Why should God choose to bless us, if we choose to disobey Him?** Malachi 3:6 says: *"For I, the Lord do not change"* NAS.

Have we asked God to heal us, deliver us, and free us from torment and at the same time refused to listen to His voice by saying to Him "Let me keep my sin, it is only a little anger and after all it is justified." You know what they did to me Lord, so it's ok to be angry and hate them. But if you are listening you will hear His still small voice that says

"No it is not ok! Forgive like your savior forgave and trust me for the outcome"

I know that these are hard questions, but we are living in an hour that we had better be serious about God's word to us and our response to His word.

Forgiveness test

How can we know that we really have forgiven?

Here are three things that I have found useful in my own life and in ministering to others.

1- **After forgiveness, are you keeping a record of wrongs against your offender?** If so, then you have not forgiven!

131

2- Do you still want to see the offender punished? If so, you have not forgiven, because you still holding them to their debt!

I saw a story on television recently where three grown sisters had been sexually molested by their father when they were children. After 30 years they had him prosecuted. He was found guilty and given a prison term that probably meant that he would die in prison because of his advanced age and failing health.

Was he guilty? Yes, he admitted his guilt and shame and asked them to forgive him. They flat refused and said in the interview that he had ruined their life and now they wanted him to pay! The TV host then asked them if they had forgiven him and their reply was "well, how can you forgive something like that?" They then added that they "were glad he was going to prison, as that is what he deserved"!

Watching and listening to the interview really broke my heart for all of these people, the father and the three sisters, because I knew that the bitterness and unforgiveness the sisters had was going to destroy them. It may already have. The father had years before given himself over to the tormentor and he had been destroyed and had done terrible damage to his children. The children were already in their forties, and I knew that it was only a matter of time till the
"red zone" living would destroy them! Watching them on TV, I knew that the enemy had already planted seeds of hate and bitterness in their hearts and that it was only a matter of time till the destruction would come with a vengeance.

Was there an answer for these three grown girls? Yes. Forgiveness and repentance was the answer, but only the grace of God will break through the 30 year old wall of hatred!

3- Total forgiveness only comes when I give up my right to tell the world what you have done to me! Wow, this is a tough one as we all love to commiserate what has happened to us! You see, when we forgive the memory of the offense may still be there, *but the pain in the memory will be gone!*

Karla's testimony

As a teaching pastor for Wellspring Ministries, Anchorage, Alaska; I taught a seminar in Kentucky during 2005. The teaching was centered on forgiveness and repentance and related issues.

Karla was the wife of the associate pastor, and she had suffered from Fibromyalgia Syndrome for five years following a horrible car accident in the year 2000. Her healing was a true miracle, and she gives credit to understanding the principles of repentance and forgiveness for that miracle!

Let her tell the story in her own words.

Dear Family and Friends,

"I want to share what the Lord has done for me.

I have had Fibromyalgia for almost 5 years. As you know, the Lord spared my life in a horrible car accident in 2000. I had been suffering chronic pain ever since. I have gone through physical therapy, surgery to remove 2 herniated discs in my neck, physical therapy again, 2 pain specialists, many prayer lines, and $1,000s of dollars of medication.

I continued to deal with severe headaches; painful, tight, muscle spasms in my neck, shoulders and back, severe joint pain, body stiffness, depression, sleeplessness, backaches; extreme exhaustion, and many more inconveniences!

Through a process of identifying sin I saw that I had been holding on to a lot of anger, resentment, unforgiveness, self hatred and bitterness from the accident, an ugly court battle over the medical bills from the acci-

dent, as well as my childhood and the death of my father.

The principles of repentance and forgiveness have set me free!

During praise I realized that I was pain free, as I could raise my arms to worship the Lord without the pain. I was in awe. I kept looking over to my left shoulder as if waiting to see if the pain was really gone or if it was going to 'show up at any second.' I have been pain free from Fibromyalgia and its ugly symptoms ever since. God is soooo... Good!!!

The healing is even more impressive due to the fact that I took Hydrocodone/Apap 10/650 at least 3-5 times daily to lessen the pain, Cyclobenzaprine, a muscle relaxer, 3-4 times a day, Trazodone, a sleep medication that only sometimes worked. I can't count the number of nights I spent up all night.

I also took Ibuprofen 800mg every 4 hours. I have been drug free ever since the seminar. People have had to go through drug rehab to get off Hydrocodone, but the Lord had healed my body of all medications and effects from them! God is soooo...Good!!!"

Karla,

Louisville, Kentucky

When I asked Karla for permission to share what the Lord had done for her, she said "Yes, please share it with anyone who is interested, as I want to always give glory and honor to the King of Kings and the Lord of Lords for the great things that He has done for me and my family." She declared "I want to always be like the one leper that returned to thank Jesus with a loud voice, not like the other nine lepers that had been healed at the same time, but did not return to give thanks!" Luke 17:11-19

John & Pam Shergur, ministers with Restoring Hearts Ministries told me that it was too bad that we did not have a "before and after" picture of Karla. John and Pam go to church with Karla and they reported that the physical change was so dramatic that she was a new woman!

To God be the glory, great things He has done!

Wow! Is God good? Yes, He is! And when we line up our thinking with His thinking the gates of heaven will open up to us and all the blessings will pour out!

Beloved, what God has done for Karla and countless folks like her, He will do for you!

God has not changed! And what He has done for Karla He will do for you! How can I be so sure? Because I have seen Him do it hundreds of times!

Steps to moving in forgiveness

The steps are found in Jesus' words in Matthew 5:44 when he said: *"Love your enemies, bless those that curse you, do good to those that hate you, and pray for those who spitefully use you and persecute you"* NKJV.

Four Spiritual Principles of Forgiveness

1- Love your enemies
2- Bless those who curse you
3- Do good to those who hate you
4- Pray for those that who spitefully use you

Are you thinking that this is impossible? God will never ask you to do anything that He will not equip you to do!

He has promised that *"With men this is impossible, but with God all things are possible"* Matthew 19:26 NKJV, and *"I can do all things through Christ who strengthens me"* Phil 4:13 NKJV, and the clincher is *"Christ in you the hope of glory"* Col. 1:27 NKJV.

The choice is yours! First choose life, then rest in the Father's lap and watch Him do wonderful things with your step of faith and obedience.

If unforgiveness or lack of repentance is causing you anguish of mind or body, then today is your day.

Beloved! Now is the day of **salvation!** Now is the day of **deliverance!** Now is the day of **healing!** Now is the day of **restoration of relationships!**

Prayer for release

If you are ready, pray with me:

Father, in Jesus name, I repent for all the resentment and bitterness, and all ungodly feelings that I have felt toward those who have abused me, hurt me, betrayed me, humiliated me or other in any way have offended me. I choose to release and forgive them from those offences.

I now ask to be forgiven for holding on to those offences that are contrary to your word. And as I have released those who have offended me, I ask to be released from my sin of unforgiveness and the offence that has caused to you Father.

Now Father, I ask you to heal me from the top of my head to the bottom of my feet and I ask to be empowered afresh and a new with your Holy Spirit!

I thank you, Father God, and I praise you,

In Jesus name, Amen!

Church, we are at war! Let's stand in the gap and get our own issues dealt with so we can help others!

RESTORING HEARTS MINISTRIES

RHM is a healing ministry founded by Ish Payne and Michael Hulsey. Their partnership brings over 60 years of combined ministry experience to the Body of Christ.

Both men have a commitment to the bring the healing ministry of our Lord and Savior to mainstream Christianity. Our "Master's Touch" healing seminars are designed to equip the believer with a strong Biblical foundation concerning healing, to help them discover the root causes of sickness, and to teach them how to minister God's healing love to others. RHM is available to come to your area.

Ish is also available to speak in churches, seminars, and conventions. He brings with him many years experience in healing ministry having prayed for and counseled thousands of people over the years.

Ish and his wife, Tonda, desire to see the gospel of the kingdom taught and manifest in the church in this hour and hold fast to the basic principle that Jesus taught in Matt 6:33.

You may contact him at:

Ish Payne
PO Box 100
Indian Trail NC 28079
ish@restoringhearts.net

Other Resources Available From
RESTORING HEARTS MINISTRIES
www.restoringhearts.net

"The Warriors Walk"
by Ish Payne

This book will address the very real issues we face in this modern world walking with the Lord!

It is a "Warrior's Walk" that brings glory and honor to the King!

Can we live in victory in the midst of trials?

*Are you a "Chocolate Soldier?"
Do you melt when the fire comes?*

Other Resources Available From

RESTORING HEARTS MINISTRIES

www.restoringhearts.net

"Guarding Your Heart's Critical Mass"

by Michael Hulsey

This timely book will cover such important topics as:

Why is the heart so important.

Know how to protect your heart from "worry overload."

What type of heart does it take to please God?

Can satan affect the heart of a believer?

Other Resources Available From
Restoring Hearts Ministries
www.restoringhearts.net

His Heart...my heart
by Melanie Hulsey
CD - $15.00

Heart...my heart" is filled with encouragement and peace. All of the songs have specific messages that we feel will touch the deep parts of the heart and bring one into His presence. "His heart...my heart" is a healing balm that reveals the love and caring heart of our Father God. This is the perfect music to play when you are needing to rest in the presence of God.

Other Resources Available From

RESTORING HEARTS MINISTRIES
www.restoringhearts.net

David's Harp
by Deanne Day
CD - $15.00

The songs on David's Harp usher in the Lord's healing presence, and peace to calm your mind, and body in these troubled times. If you experience depression, fear, bitterness or misplaced expectations, or if you have been verbally, emotionally, physically, or sexually abused, or if you just need peace from the troubled world in which we live, then this music will bring times of refreshing and healing to your life.

Books by Deanne Day

"Sifted Like Wheat"
Turning PRIDE Into PROMOTION Through REPENTANCE

Once we become born again we are in a spiritual war. Satan desires to sift us like wheat, but what does that mean? How does that happen? What does that look like in our everyday lifes? And importantly, what cand I do to prevent being sifted?

"Accusing Spirits, Judging, & Witchcraft"
Are you always feeling guilty? Then the message of Accusing Spirits who accuse you day and night have succeeded in getting you to agree with them. Do you have a hard time resting and relaxing? Do you feel driven, and guilty if you are not productive? These, and others, are tell-tale signs that you are being harassed by Accusing Spirits, and you have come into agreement with their lies.

143